# First World War
and Army of Occupation
# War Diary
France, Belgium and Germany

3 INDIAN (LAHORE) DIVISION
Divisional Troops
Royal Army Medical Corps
112 Indian Field Ambulance
1 January 1914 - 29 December 1915

WO95/3920/4

The Naval & Military Press Ltd
www.nmarchive.com
Published in association with The National Archives

Published by

## The Naval & Military Press Ltd

Unit 10 Ridgewood Industrial Park,

Uckfield, East Sussex,

TN22 5QE England

Tel: +44 (0) 1825 749494

www.naval-military-press.com

www.nmarchive.com

*This diary has been reprinted in facsimile from the original. Any imperfections are inevitably reproduced and the quality may fall short of modern type and cartographic standards.*

© **Crown Copyright**
**Images reproduced by permission of The National Archives, London, England, 2015.**

# Contents

| Document type | Place/Title | Date From | Date To |
|---|---|---|---|
| Heading | WO95/3920/4 | | |
| Heading | BEF 3 Ind Lahore Div Troops 1/2 Indian Fld Amb 1914 Aug-1915 Dec. | | |
| War Diary | Lahore Cantonment | 10/08/1914 | 15/08/1914 |
| War Diary | Karachi | 16/08/1914 | 13/09/1914 |
| War Diary | Suez | 14/08/1914 | 16/09/1914 |
| War Diary | Alexandria | 17/08/1914 | 25/09/1914 |
| War Diary | Marseilles | 26/09/1914 | 03/10/1914 |
| War Diary | Orleans | 04/10/1914 | 25/10/1914 |
| War Diary | Lagorgue | 26/10/1914 | 31/10/1914 |
| Heading | No112 Ind F.A. | | |
| War Diary | Noo La Gorgue | 01/01/1914 | 15/01/1914 |
| War Diary | Zelobes | 16/11/1915 | 21/11/1915 |
| War Diary | Selingues | 23/11/1915 | 29/11/1915 |
| Heading | War Diary No. 112 Ind F.A Dec 1914 | | |
| Heading | Salonica History 18d (C.C.S) | | |
| War Diary | Selingues | 01/12/1914 | 01/12/1914 |
| War Diary | Bethune | 10/12/1914 | 10/12/1914 |
| War Diary | Beuvry | 11/12/1914 | 15/12/1914 |
| War Diary | Bethune | 16/12/1914 | 22/12/1914 |
| War Diary | Raimbert | 23/12/1914 | 31/12/1914 |
| Miscellaneous | Copy of Telegram 618/29 Dated 8.8.14. Appendix 1 | | |
| Heading | War Diary 112th Indian Field Ambulance Lahore Division. From 1st January 1915 To 31st January 1915 | | |
| Heading | 112 Indian Field Ambulance Lahore Division L. E.F. January 1st To 31st 1915 | | |
| War Diary | Rembert | 01/01/1915 | 13/01/1915 |
| War Diary | Vielle Chapelle | 14/01/1915 | 14/01/1915 |
| War Diary | Lacouture | 15/01/1915 | 15/01/1915 |
| War Diary | Zelobes | 16/01/1915 | 16/01/1915 |
| War Diary | Paradis | 17/01/1915 | 21/01/1915 |
| War Diary | Raimbert | 22/01/1915 | 30/01/1915 |
| War Diary | Lozinghem | 31/01/1915 | 31/01/1915 |
| Heading | War Diary 112 Indian Ambulance Lahore Division From 1st February To 28th February | | |
| War Diary | Calonne | 01/02/1915 | 09/02/1915 |
| War Diary | Locon | 10/02/1915 | 22/02/1915 |
| War Diary | Calonne | 23/02/1915 | 28/02/1915 |
| Heading | War Diary With Appendices 112 Indian Field Ambulance Lahore Division From 1st March 1915 To 1915 31st March 1915 | | |
| Heading | 112 Indian Field Ambulance Lahore Division I.e.f. March 1st To 31st 1915 | | |
| War Diary | Calonne | 01/03/1915 | 12/03/1915 |
| War Diary | Zelobes | 13/03/1915 | 30/03/1915 |
| Miscellaneous | War Diary 112 I.F.A. Appendix 1 | | |
| Miscellaneous | War Diary 112 I.F.A. Appendix 2 | 17/03/1915 | 17/03/1915 |
| Miscellaneous | War Diary 112 I.F.A. Appendix 3. | 19/03/1915 | 19/03/1915 |
| Miscellaneous | | 18/03/1915 | 18/03/1915 |

| | | | |
|---|---|---|---|
| Heading | War Diary With Appendices. Lahore Division From 1st April 1915 To 30th April 1915 30th April 1915 | | |
| War Diary | Robecq | 01/04/1915 | 24/04/1915 |
| War Diary | Kruystraete | 25/04/1915 | 25/04/1915 |
| War Diary | Vlamertinghe | 26/04/1915 | 30/04/1915 |
| Heading | War Diary of 112th Indian Field Ambulance Lahore Division From 1st May 1915 To 31st May 1915 | | |
| Heading | 112 Indian Filed Ambulance Lahore Division May 1st To 31st 1915 | | |
| War Diary | Boeschepe | 01/05/1915 | 02/05/1915 |
| War Diary | Calonne | 03/05/1915 | 06/05/1915 |
| War Diary | Croix Marmuse | 07/05/1915 | 23/05/1915 |
| War Diary | Sq Riqa | 23/05/1915 | 30/05/1915 |
| War Diary | La Gorgue | 31/05/1915 | 31/05/1915 |
| Miscellaneous | O.C. 102 I.F.A. Appendix 4 | 01/05/1915 | 01/05/1915 |
| Miscellaneous | War Diary 112 I.F.A. Appendix 5 | 02/05/1915 | 02/05/1915 |
| War Diary | Lahore Division I.e.f. June 1st To 30th 1915 | | |
| Miscellaneous | A Form, Messages And Signals | | |
| Miscellaneous | Correspondence on Good work done under shell Fire by Man of No.112 I.F.A. on June 12.1915. Appendix 7 | 07/06/1915 | 07/06/1915 |
| War Diary | Lagorgue | 01/06/1915 | 30/06/1915 |
| Miscellaneous | Points Diary June April | | |
| Heading | War Diary of 112 Indian Field Ambulance From 1st July 1915 to 31st July 1915 | | |
| War Diary | La Gorgue | 01/07/1915 | 31/07/1915 |
| Heading | War Diary of 112 Indian Field Ambulance Lahore Lahore Division From 1st August 1915 To 31st 1915 | | |
| War Diary | La Gorgue | 01/08/1915 | 27/08/1915 |
| War Diary | Calonne | 28/08/1915 | 31/08/1915 |
| Heading | War Diary of 112th Indian Field Ambulance From 1st September 1915 To 30th September 1915 | | |
| War Diary | Calonne | 01/09/1915 | 22/09/1915 |
| War Diary | Croix Marmuse | 23/09/1915 | 30/09/1915 |
| Heading | War Diary of No.112 Indian Field Ambulance From 1st October 1915 To 31st October | | |
| Heading | 112 Indian Field Ambulance Lahore October 1915 | | |
| War Diary | Croix Marmuse | 01/10/1915 | 03/10/1915 |
| War Diary | La Gorgue L34 B. 103 | 04/10/1915 | 31/10/1915 |
| Heading | 112 Indian Field Ambulance Lahore Divn November 1915 | | |
| War Diary | La Gorgue | 01/11/1915 | 08/11/1915 |
| War Diary | Ham En Artois | 09/11/1915 | 17/11/1915 |
| War Diary | Enguinegatte | 18/11/1915 | 28/11/1915 |
| War Diary | Beaumetz-Les-Aire | 29/11/1915 | 30/11/1915 |
| Heading | 112 Ind Field Ambulance Lahore Div Dec 1915 | | |
| Heading | Cover for Documents. Nature of Enclosures X-Ray Salonica History 18th | | |
| Heading | 112 Indian Filed Ambulance Lahore Division December 1915 | | |
| War Diary | Beaumetz Aries | 01/12/1915 | 01/12/1915 |
| War Diary | Amettes | 01/12/1915 | 14/12/1915 |
| War Diary | Marseilles | 15/12/1915 | 18/12/1915 |
| War Diary | Voyage | 19/12/1915 | 29/12/1915 |

No 003/3020/14

BEF

3 IND LAHORE DIV TROOPS

112 INDIAN FLD AMB

1914 AUG — 1915 DEC

To MESOPOTAMIA

112 IND FLD AMB Army Form C. 2118.

Page 1.

# WAR DIARY
or
## INTELLIGENCE SUMMARY.
(Erase heading not required.)

| Hour, Date, Place. | Summary of Events and Information. | Remarks and references to Appendices. |
|---|---|---|
| 7.0 A.M. 10.8.14. LAHORE CANTONMENT | In accordance with Telegram 616/29. 8.8.14 from ADMS 3rd Divn to O.C. LAHORE CANTONMENT commenced mobilization of No 112 I.F.A. Sub Assistant Surgeons NARAYAN PERSHAD SUKUL — KANIYA LAL — GOKAL SINGH — SUDAMA RAM — SHEIKH ALI JAN Four peons, Six Kaherdars from Calcutta, one 1st class storekeeper one assist storekeeper, Sergt WATKINS SGT (for Dempsey absent) reported their arrivals for duty with unit. | Telegram 616/29 (copy) Appendix 1. |
| 11.8.14 | Continued mobilization. Senior Sub assist Surgn — GAOR SHANKAR S.A.S India Singh. 1 peon 1 ward orderlies one labourer and four sweepers updated their arrival for duty with unit. | |
| 12.8.14. | Continued mobilization assisted by Major KEATES IMS and Captain REINHOLD IMS. SAS KANIYA LAL transferred to 111 I.F.A and SAS WARYAM SINGH joined this unit in his place. Two ward orderlies, two Kaherdis and one cook joined their arrivals for duty. | |
| 13.8.14 | Mobilization completed as the unit was transferred to the 26th Punjabis | |

Army Form C. 2118.

Page 2.

# WAR DIARY
## or
## INTELLIGENCE SUMMARY.
(Erase heading not required.)

Instructions regarding War Diaries and Intelligence Summaries are contained in F. S. Regs., Part II, and the Staff Manual respectively. Title pages will be prepared in manuscript.

| Hour, Date, Place. | Summary of Events and Information. | Remarks and references to Appendices. |
|---|---|---|
| LAHORE CANTONMENT 13.8.14 | Two went detailed as Ass Sweepers refused their services for duty | |
| | The Army Bearer Personnel attached from this date. | |
| 7.0 PM. 14.8.14. | Unit inspected by ADMS 3rd Division. Lieut P.J. WALSH I.M.S. S.A.S. BALA RAM refused their services for duty. S.A.S. WARYAM SINGH found unfit for active service | |
| 15.8.14. | Major H.M.H. MELHUISH – Captain J.F. BOYD I.M.S. S.a.S. RAM KISHEN ANANT PARAB and one 2nd grade Storekeeper refused their services for duty with the Unit | |
| | The unit entrained at LAHORE CANTT. W. | |
| 16.30 AM " | On main journey. Rations on route. | |
| KARACHI. 16.8.14. 9.30 AM 17.8.14. | Arrived Karachi and proceeded to the Staging Camp. One cook and two bhistis refused their services for duty. | |
| KARACHI 18.8.14 | Personnel detailed to Sections and paraded as such. | |
| " 19.8.14 | Bearer Company detailed and paraded under command of Major H.M.H. MELHUISH. Divisional Orders X in station to all ranks. | |

Gulab Singh & Sons, Calcutta—No. 22 Army C.—5·8·14—1,07,000.

Army Form C. 2118.

Page 3.

# WAR DIARY
## or
## INTELLIGENCE SUMMARY.
*(Erase heading not required.)*

Instructions regarding War Diaries and Intelligence Summaries are contained in F. S. Regs., Part II, and the Staff Manual respectively. Title pages will be prepared in manuscript.

| Hour, Date, Place. | Summary of Events and Information. | Remarks and references to Appendices. |
|---|---|---|
| 20 <br> 21.8.14. KARACHI. | Company drill & Stretcher drill Carried out with tent poles as stretchers as available in KARACHI. The Jeersing Amphalies (sent to Camp CELLIA PULCHERRIMA at N.STEPHENSI. Drive 9/s I in Section gun to all Ranks. | |
| 24.8.14.  " | Drill etc as above. (Note) Some of the hospital lamps are marked for dimmings (no spare lamps been issued in exchange was made to obtain Oxidly Oil not suitable nor could it be got. | |
| 22.8.14.  " | Drill etc as above. A lecture to S.A. Sergrs. on General work to Fuel Autobuses given by O.C. Drive 9/s I to all Ranks. | |
| 23.8.14.  " | Sunday. | |
| 24.8.14.  " | Drill & instruct to personnel, Drive 9/s I to all Ranks. | |
| 25 & 26.8.14. | As above. | |
| 27.8.14. | Warned to be ready to move at very short notice after midday. | |
| 11.0 AM. 28.8.14. | Telephone message from Cheadlass-Officer with orders to embark arrived at 1.30 PM arrival at Kaimari Dock at 3.15 PM. at 7.45 PM commenced to put equipment on to S.S. CASTALIA. All equipment & personnel on board at 12.15 midnight. The equipment could not be kept separately in the hold as other equipment previously occupied all floor space. | |

Gulab Singh & Sons, Calcutta.—No. 22 A.D.—C.T.SGA—1,07,000. 9.h. mfs all filler space.

Army Form C. 2118.

# WAR DIARY
or
# INTELLIGENCE SUMMARY.

(Erase heading not required.)

Page 4.

Instructions regarding War Diaries and Intelligence Summaries are contained in F. S. Regs., Part II, and the Staff Manual respectively. Title pages will be prepared in manuscript.

| Hour, Date, Place. | Summary of Events and Information. | Remarks and references to Appendices. |
|---|---|---|
| 1.30 PM 29.8.14. KARACHI. | Lipt Rankin. Personnel accommodated in No 1 hold. Space & ventilation appear satisfactory. Heavy sweet journey. | |
| At Sea. 30.8.14. | Practically all personnel sea sick. With exception of B.O.s & S.a.S GAUR SHANKAR. | |
| 31.8.14 | Ditto | |
| 1.9.14 | Men feeling those able to do so exercised on upper deck. | |
| " 2-3-9-14. | Ditto | |
| 4.9.14. | All personnel now fit. Major BROWSE & Lt WALSH inoculated against enteric. | |
| 5-6.9.14. | Ditto | |
| 7.9.14. | Arrived Aden left same evening. | |
| 8.9.14 | Four men specially selected from each Section leave company, these men will be individually placed doing duty & further practice in Aerial & Visual Section Communications. They will act as instructors to their Sections. | |
| " 9-10-11-12.9.14 | Routine exercise & general instruction duty to all Ranks. | |

Gulab Singh & Sons, Calcutta.—No. 22 Army C.—5-8-14—1,07,000.

Army Form C. 2118.

Page 5.

# WAR DIARY
## or
## INTELLIGENCE SUMMARY.
(Erase heading not required.)

Instructions regarding War Diaries and Intelligence Summaries are contained in F. S. Regs., Part II, and the Staff Manual respectively. Title pages will be prepared in manuscript.

| Hour, Date, Place. | Summary of Events and Information. | Remarks and references to Appendices. |
|---|---|---|
| 13.9.14 | Arrived SUEZ at 4.0 P.M. | |
| 14.9.14 SUEZ | Holiday. | |
| 15.9.14 | Left SUEZ 9.0 A.M. Exercise & instruction all ranks. Arrived PORT SAID 8.0 P.M. | |
| 16.9.14 | Left PORT SAID 8.0 A.M. Arrived ALEXANDRIA 9.0 P.M. | |
| 17.9.14 ALEXANDRIA | Took personnel for route march, which was quite satisfactory. | |
| 18.9.14 " | Shelter drill on S.S. Routine. | |
| 19.9.14 | Left ALEXANDRIA at noon. Majors BROWSE – MELHUISH & Captn. | |
|  | BOYD inoculated against enteric. | |
| 20-21-22-23-24.9.14 | Routine. | |
| 25 | Arrived at Marseilles 10.30 A.M. Commenced unloading at 8.30 P.M. Coffee 10.30 P.M. | |
| MARSEILLES 26.9.14 | Bivouaced on Quay. Marched to Camp at Parc Borely. | |
| 27.9.14 | Route marches & routine. All personnel left in Camp unless on duty. | |
| 28.29.9.14 | Camp to Gare D'Arenc 2.10 to 3.45 P.M. Train left at 6.15 P.M | |
| 30.9.14 | | |
| Oct 1.2.14 | Train journey. 3 Army beds daily with shorter stops | |
| 3.10.14 | Arrived ORLEANS midnight. Detrained & marched Camp 3.0 A.M. Bivouaced. | |
|  | Pitched Camp at dawn | |

Gulab Singh & Sons, Calcutta—No. 22 Army C.—5-8-14—1,07,000.

Army Form C. 2118.

PAGE 6.

# WAR DIARY
## or
## INTELLIGENCE SUMMARY.
*(Erase heading not required.)*

Instructions regarding War Diaries and Intelligence Summaries are contained in F. S. Regs., Part II, and the Staff Manual respectively. Title pages will be prepared in manuscript.

| Hour, Date, Place. | Summary of Events and Information. | Remarks and references to Appendices. |
|---|---|---|
| ORLEANS, Oct 4, 1914 | Route march. | |
| " 5 " | Parkhampscathdown, opened a section to take in sick. | |
| " 6 " | Route march. Practice – loaded ambulance wagons 6 of which have been | |
| " 6 " | taken over by A.S.C. | |
| " 6 " | Bearer party under Major Hellwith marched off 9 funds a dressing Station | |
| | 9 collected dummy wounded | |
| | Sketch of load drive. | |
| " 7 " | Bearer arty practice as on 6th | |
| " 8 " | Drill & Gudies | |
| " 9 " | Bearer arty practice as on 6th. | |
| " 10 " | Practice | |
| " 11 " | Pte Major G. BROUSE transferred sick to No 10 Stationary Hospital | a/s |
| " 21 " | | |

Army Form C. 2118.

Page 2

# WAR DIARY
## or
## INTELLIGENCE SUMMARY.
*(Erase heading not required.)*

| Hour, Date, Place. | Summary of Events and Information. | Remarks and references to Appendices. |
|---|---|---|
| 12-6-14 ORLÉANS | MAJOR BROWNE transferred sick to No 16 Stationary Hospital; Command of the Unit taken over by Major H. MELHUISH. Routine parades. Weather excellent all 13.10.14. | |
| 13.10.14 | Kit-inspection – all private kit of Bearers followers packed in separate bundles & marked with owners name to be left behind at Base, & assumed again on return with them. Superintendent according to scale. Kit drawn from Ordnance. Useful appearance since on arrival in France. | |
| 14.10.14. | Camp Routine. | |
| 15.10.14. | Surplus Kit of personnel left with Unit Base. Sgts: Bradford & Infantry. | |
| 16.10.14. | & Ambulances ordered for escort out. | |
| 17.10.14. | Transferred 42 followers to No 10 Stationary & G team, Standing fast for orders to return. | |

Army Form C. 2118.

Page 8

# WAR DIARY
## or
## INTELLIGENCE SUMMARY.
*(Erase heading not required.)*

| Hour, Date, Place. | Summary of Events and Information. | Remarks and references to Appendices. |
|---|---|---|
| 18-10-14 Orleans | The Field Ambulance entrained at 7.55pm during station. On the road 15 Nastern Bruce No 433 W Nathan fell off his waggon hurts himself. He was placed on a stately information outside No 10 Stationary Hospital to fetch him from the station. | |
| 19-10-14 | Train Journey continues thro' Juvisy + Rouen to Etaples reached at 7.45 A.m. Orders received there be continuing the journey to BLANDECQUES. | |
| 20-10-14 | BOULOGNE passed at 11 am – CALAIS reached at 10 am + BLANDECQUES at 12 noon – detraining | SM |

**Army Form C. 2118**

Pay 9

# WAR DIARY
## or
## INTELLIGENCE SUMMARY.
*(Erase heading not required.)*

| Hour, Date, Place. | Summary of Events and Information. | Remarks and references to Appendices. |
|---|---|---|
| 21-10-14 | Reconnoitred in 9½ Rcars – Ambulance marched at 3 p.m. to LOMBRES via WIZERNE + HALINES – Arrived at 8 p.m. + billeted in a large hall – Accommodation sufficient. Weather raining. Relief descent cool. Marched from LOMBRES to EBBLINGHAM Started at 2 p.m. + arrived 9 p.m. Owing to the distance + our billeting area from the remainder of the Division, & locations at which our orders were received (2:30 p.m.) it was impossible for the 2 Camb. Water Carts to keep place in the Column, so we marched without them. Two Ambulances wagons were collided with a heavy lorry & left behind the Heavy Battery, Grenmine at EBBLINGHAM We found on arrival that they had been taken by a party | MAP SET A. STOMER |

Army Form C. 2118.

Page 10

# WAR DIARY
or
# INTELLIGENCE SUMMARY.

(Erase heading not required.)

| Hour, Date, Place. | Summary of Events and Information. | Remarks and references to Appendices. |
|---|---|---|
| | of the 15th Sikhs. She heller was reported to the Colonel of the regiment who refused to harbour his men - one man was subsequently killed was a Good shot at the railway station. She 5 figures dialects were those of 1st SWEET of 113 I.F.A. in the presence of an officer of the 15th Sikhs thanked for our hospitality. No rations required for higher days. Two ambulance waggons sent to join the units. | |
| 23-10-14 | E.B.B.L.I.N.G.H.A.M to HAZEBROUCK marched at 10 A.M - arrived at 2.30 P.M. Billeted in a market; accommodation very Good. Lt WALSH with two mule carts joined (2) one day's rations from WARDRECKS. Weather fairly warm | MAP SET A. STOMER |

Army Form C. 2118.

Page 11

# WAR DIARY
## or
## INTELLIGENCE SUMMARY.
(Erase heading not required.)

| Hour, Date, Place. | Summary of Events and Information. | Remarks and references to Appendices. |
|---|---|---|
| 23.10.14 | HAZEBROUCK to LES DRUMEZ via MERVILLE, LA GORGUE & ESTAIRS. Marched at 9 AM and arrived 1 P.M. Billets in a decided farm house. Every man to go for his own rations. Being necessarily unfavourable. No Divisional Column, being 15th was scattered over an area on which the troops are billeted. At LES DRUMEZ. Horses (half) offered for sale. Two ambulances half a mile were sent forward at LUMBRES, 19 miles away. | MAP SET A. ST OMER |
| 24-10-14 | Half the Bearer Division under Lt W.H.Sh. went forward in the direction of LAVENTIE to form a dressing station. Company with half the Bearer Division of No 6 B.F.A. under Major GIBSON R.A.M.C. "A" section took cold water. | |

# WAR DIARY
## or
## INTELLIGENCE SUMMARY.

Army Form C. 2118.

Day 12

(Erase heading not required.)

| Hour, Date, Place. | Summary of Events and Information. | Remarks and references to Appendices. |
|---|---|---|
| | Stayed at LES DRUMEZ under CAPT BOYD to receive the wounded. Sgt BOYD certified from two ambulances positions occupied from two of ambulances to a mile & a quarter along the road from NEUVE-CHAPELLE to FLEURBAUX northeast of FAUQUISSART. The remainder of the ambulances under MAJOR MELHUISH marched to LOCON via ESTAIRS + GORGUE + LA coming Near at 7 Pu & billeting in-farmery loft. No 8 British G-A-  The dressing station has formed field had was ordered shave Sheet Rome to land of LAVENTIE hut at the commencement of shell fire on the farm the Sewen Bearers retired on LES DRUMEZ | MAP SET A ARRAS |

Army Form C. 2118.

Page 13

# WAR DIARY
## or
## INTELLIGENCE SUMMARY.
*(Erase heading not required.)*

Instructions regarding War Diaries and Intelligence Summaries are contained in F. S. Regs., Part II, and the Staff Manual respectively. Title pages will be prepared in manuscript.

| Hour, Date, Place. | Summary of Events and Information. | Remarks and references to Appendices. |
|---|---|---|
| 25-10-14. | Subsequently Capt. BOYD went out with a patrol of the Seven Browns and myself in two motors to LES DRUMEZ, after which the Seven Browns + two section was withdrawn to LA GORGUE, about a mile from ESTAIRES, where they were billeted in a school on the main road to BETHUNE.<br><br>"A" Section under Capt BOYD opened at terrain wounded in the above school buildings at LA GORGUE, Al-NAHSH being adjoining the 39 Severn Bn in billets. Wounded from LAVENTIE.<br>In the afternoon MAJOR MELDISH with the Head Quarters & (B.C.D) sections at LOCON received orders to return to LA GORGUE taking with him [billets?] ambulance wagons. | MAP SET A<br>SHEET<br>LM. |

Army Form C. 2118.

Page 14

# WAR DIARY
## or
## INTELLIGENCE SUMMARY.
*(Erase heading not required.)*

| Hour, Date, Place. | Summary of Events and Information. | Remarks and references to Appendices. |
|---|---|---|
| 26-10-14<br>LAGORGUE | Tears each from Nos 1 & 3 F. Ambulances. He arrived here at 7pm. CAPT BOYD then returned with the remainder of the 7th Meerut Division + two ambulances to join the Brigade situated at Ta? Justingion. the Brigade situated at a village called PICANTIN. Preparations for the reception of wounded were completed by MAJOR MELHUISH, Patients brought in later by CAPT BOYD + LIEUT WALSH were dressed + disposed of in the wards—in the way 13 patients were admitted the majority being completed at 7am on the 26th.<br>The Field Ambulance Journées open for Worcesters, Wounded & Sick. The building is used as a School in times of peace. | |

Army Form C. 2118.

Nov 15

# WAR DIARY
## or
## INTELLIGENCE SUMMARY.
*(Erase heading not required.)*

| Hour, Date, Place. | Summary of Events and Information. | Remarks and references to Appendices. |
|---|---|---|
| | Peace remarks of a hain regimental block of 3 storeys. A block of 3 class rooms behind with a central corridor welcoming hall. The three class rooms was utilised when capable of holding about 30 patients. In the centre one room were selected for the reception of patients on account of proximity to dressing rooms & for office or as we also supposed, lavatories & c. Palaces, dining room & pantry in the central block. An office was also situated for a kitchen behind the main block. Patients brought in by ambulances during the day were treated in the evening. CpT Boyd with six ambulances no fore & half the Bearer Company returned to the [?] and part of the 15 [?] field [?] 47 K [?] + 345 [?] + collected these | [signature] |

**Army Form C. 2118.**

Pg 6

# WAR DIARY
## or
## INTELLIGENCE SUMMARY.
*(Erase heading not required.)*

Instructions regarding War Diaries and Intelligence Summaries are contained in F. S. Regs., Part II, and the Staff Manual respectively. Title pages will be prepared in manuscript.

| Hour, Date, Place. | Summary of Events and Information. | Remarks and references to Appendices. |
|---|---|---|
| 26-10-14. | wounded. Arrived at the Rateaulchamère [?] here & crossed river at ford & set to work procuring Lieut NALSH & Lieut McLNTOSH brought me all [?] the horses & ambulance being regimental carts. With the regiment I started off & much time was lost clearing the letters of an difficult spot between the ambulance & the horses lines, till about [?] half of [?] each cart was loaded with wounded men until all his bourn [?] were collected [ ] another mile on met. Work proceeded to Estaires — turning the day. 111 wounded men were evacuated & dressed here & work of collecting them from the regimental carts being carried out after dark by Lieut NALSH with the ambulance | Sd/ |

Army Form C. 2118.

Copy 17

# WAR DIARY
## or
## INTELLIGENCE SUMMARY.

(Erase heading not required.)

| Hour, Date, Place. | Summary of Events and Information. | Remarks and references to Appendices. |
|---|---|---|
| 26-10-14 | Hoffer & Braun Company. Fifty four wounded were evacuated during morning to No. 15 Clearing Hospital at Bailleul in motor ambulances provided by the British Red Cross Society. Weather clear with rain. Heavy firing. Company remains very good. | |
| | Lifts for massages was omitted. Hospital to mark stretchers from refused cases at LT-WALSH - to lay again informed to the historical ambulances. Numbers evacuated during time cost from having reported to himself. Refusing quite to Henri Chapelle where a military Hospital. Place houses are still in reference to by Saffron Minions. 2nd Shehad Infantry (their eyes the Engers Well over the high belief above. Quite noticeable features. | [signature] |

# WAR DIARY
## or
## INTELLIGENCE SUMMARY.
*(Erase heading not required.)*

Army Form C. 2118.

Oct 18

| Hour, Date, Place. | Summary of Events and Information. | Remarks and references to Appendices. |
|---|---|---|
| 29-10-14- | The casualties admitted have been the cause of infantry officers wounded, the Coldstream and Grenadier wounds — the Irish Guards 1 50% company, 15 of 26 wounded after returning to that of infantry — S.A.S.C. Ali Jan & Shei Singh with Fd Bearer were detailed for special duty, orders fluctuating further orders. Eighty four field cases were admitted, ten have been evacuated the previous day. The accommodation was arranged for school in the Rue de Richelieu. Later in the day 16 Cav Cases were evacuated to 15 Clearing Hospital & to be held in reserve for the field station receiving patients till further orders. MAJOR BROWSE I.M.S. returned by return train from No. 10 Stationary Hospital Orleans. I took over command of the Field Ambulance. | SW |

Army Form C. 2118.

# WAR DIARY
## or
## INTELLIGENCE SUMMARY.
(Erase heading not required.)

Page 19

| Hour, Date, Place. | Summary of Events and Information. | Remarks and references to Appendices. |
|---|---|---|
| Oct 30.1914 LA GORGUE. | All wounded evacuated to clearing hospital by motor ambulances. 13 wounded and 6 Sick admitted. Lieut WALSH proceeded at dusk with ambulance waggons & bearers to LE DRUMEZ to form a dressing station and from there collect wounded from Seginated and posts. | MAP SET A ST OMER |
| Oct 31. " | 1 wounded 5 Sick admitted during the 24 hours (midnight to midnight) Captain BOYD proceeded to LE DRUMEZ with 1/2 Bearer Company. | |
| November 1 " | 20 wounded 16 Sick admitted. All wounded evacuated during the day. A Sub Assistant Surgeon and Ward Orderly with 30 A.B.C. men remain at LE DRUMEZ during the day. Lt WALSH proceeded with the waggons and remainder of men etc to make the 1/2 Bearer Company at dusk to Hd place. | |
| " 2 " | 24 wounded and 3 Sick admitted 21 wounded & 12 Sick evacuated. Captain BOYD proceeded at 4.0 P.M. to LE DRUMEZ with Complement of establishment as before. Major W.H. ODLUM joined his unit for duty. | |
| " 3rd " | Lt WALSH out with Bearer Compy. 13 wounded & 4 Sick admitted | |
| " 4th " | Maj MELHUISH ditto 8 " 12 " O.C. sick and posts | |
| " 5th " | Maj ODLUM ditto 5 " 9 " | |
| " 6th " | Capt BOYD ditto 16 " 26 " | |
| " 7 " | Lt WALSH ditto 36 " 6 " | |

# WAR DIARY
## or
## INTELLIGENCE SUMMARY.

Army Form C. 2118.

*(Erase heading not required.)*

| Hour, Date, Place. | Summary of Events and Information. | Remarks and references to Appendices. |
|---|---|---|

**1914**
**Nov.**
**LA GORGUE**

General mode of all aspects at La Gorgue.

The Ambulance is billetted in the Municipal Boys' school the rooms of which are utilised as in the simple plan in margin: The yard & filled line in the covered sheds, offices & medical subordinates in the upstair rooms. The rooms had evidently been ransacked by the enemy & any article of value. Furniture etc was collected & locked up in one of the upstair rooms. A N/O was detailed for charge of medical cases (Major MELHUISH) and Surgical cases (Captain Boyd) and a definite staff allotted & given to the Office, Operating room, Receiving Room & Dressing Room. In the Receiving Room cases were written up in the admission & discharge book at a Transfer Return made up. They are then passed along as required to either the Operating or dressing room or direct to ward. The S of S on duty for the day sees that last milk, sub stimulants etc are given to the patients as ordered by the B.O. in return on condition of patient, Operations etc etc so that a second will go on with the patient when such is necessary. —

The arrangements for the collection of wounded are as follows —

*[Margin diagram showing layout: Road to Estaires, with Shed, Office, Receiving/Dressing Room, Court Yard, Beds, and Class Rooms occupied by Sick & wounded]*

Army Form C. 2118.

Pag 21.

# WAR DIARY
## or
## INTELLIGENCE SUMMARY.
*(Erase heading not required.)*

Instructions regarding War Diaries and Intelligence Summaries are contained in F. S. Regs., Part II, and the Staff Manual respectively. Title pages will be prepared in manuscript.

| Hour, Date, Place. | Summary of Events and Information. | Remarks and references to Appendices. |
|---|---|---|

Arrangements for collection of wounded —
An advanced dressing station is found about 1½ miles from the trenches and the same distance from the building occupied by the ambulance. At this spot a S.A.S. with hand orderly 20 A/BC men and equipment for 12 bearer division remain. At dusk a M.O. with horse ambulance, S.C.S. at the remainder of the personnel of the ½ bearer division, is sent from the Ambulance & proceeds to a rendezvous about ¾ mile from the trenches, here he is met by representatives of each regiment from which wounded are to be collected, these men show him the various regimental aid posts. A S.A.S. remains with the wagons at the rendezvous until just before dawn. From the advanced dress. station the wounded are brought back to the ambulance in motor ambulances.
From the Ambulance the wounded are evacuated to Jailhead by Red Cross motor ambulances daily.

Trenches 8th LA GORGUE. Major ODLUM proceeded & with the Bearer Coy J (night of 8-9.)

" 9th "     ditto
" 10th "    3rd wound of Sick admitted 18 " 5 " " (nights of 9-10)
" 11th "   Lieut WALSH  ditto  3 " " " (night 10-11)
" 12th "   Maj. MELHUISH ditto   6 " 0 " Hospital Church for wounded
" 13-14-15 "  Captn. BOYD — Lieut WALSH — Major MELHUISH COLLETT killed on their nights
                                        ODLUM

CWS

Army Form C. 2118.

Page 22.

# WAR DIARY
## or
## INTELLIGENCE SUMMARY.

(Erase heading not required.)

| Hour, Date, Place. | Summary of Events and Information. | Remarks and references to Appendices. |
|---|---|---|
| November 16. ZELOBES | Arrived by first train 2.0 to 4.0 P.M. opened to receive Sick. Few Billets, a Congo Bay left for Sick. A.B.C. been below. S.A.S from 8th Dgn. Officers in inn opposite. Two motor ambulances attached (for general duty in Division) | MAP SET A. St OMER |
| 17 | Hard frost. Made straw mattresses by sorry spare blankets, patients say warm & comfortable | |
| 18 | Snow about 2 inches. Frost continues. 20th Heavy M.M. all day. Clear & bright Sun. | |
| 19 | | |
| 21 | Frost continues, a few large shells fell at back of billet (about 300 yds) about midnight. 22nd Weather as above. | |
| 23 SELINQUES | Arrived by first train 1.0 to 3.0 P.M. P.M. Billet, shells at back (some half for wounded, a Congo Room upstairs made sufficiently warm for abt 22 able to got up a steep flight of stairs. Stretcher cases in huts. E.A.S in room off the ward. B.D.S in huts. A.B.C. men in a barn close front to BETHUNE. Thursday night Captain J.F.Boyd transferred to clearing hospital with Fever & Jaundice. | MAP SET A. ARRAS |
| 25" " | Open to receive Sick & wounded. Lieut 26th Mulls of made. Collecting for aid posts. Lieut P.S.WALSH from 57th Rifles as a temporary measure. Lieut SWEET from 113 I.F.A. joined for temporary duty. Collecting for aid posts. | |
| 26" — | 0.0 Visited required aid posts. Took 1½ hours from time of leaving F.A. to time of return to advanced dressing Station (with 2 cases) 27th Mulls made. Artillery afternoon. | |
| 27" " | Lieut W.S.PATON MDets Lie aimed in place of Captain BOYD. Collecting aid posts. | |
| 28" " | died P.J.WALSH returned & did SWEET rejoined 113 I.F.A. Collecting for aid posts. | |
| 29" " | Mulls of made. Collecting for aid posts. | |

Van Dray.
No. 112 2nd. F. A.
Dec. 1916

Dec.
1916

Salonica (C.C.S)

History 18 D.

No. 112. 9. 7 Army Form C. 2118.

Page 23.

# WAR DIARY
## or
## INTELLIGENCE SUMMARY.
*(Erase heading not required.)*

| Hour, Date, Place. | Summary of Events and Information. | Remarks and references to Appendices. |
|---|---|---|
| SELINGUES, Dec 1st 2nd & 3rd 1914 | Orders to rest – collecting work for Ord posts, Coal night under usual arrangements. | |
| Dec. 4th | Stafford Orderly wounded. Day collection of Sick. | |
| 5th | Major ODLUM detached for disinfection duty under A.D.M.S. | |
| " 6.7.8th | Day collection of Sick. | |
| BETHUNE 10th | Major MELHUISH left on 7 days leave. The F.A. left SELINGUES & opened up at BETHUNE in Sommary which made a very good Hospital building. Maj KENNEDY joined from III F.A. for heavy duty. | MAP. SET A ARRAS |
| BEUVRY 11th | 4th BETHUNE at once arrived at Buys relieved at 1.0 and found it occupied by French troops who did not evacuate till 3.30 P.M. The surveys of the building in a highly insanitary condition little better than an open latrine, the houses occupied being made no attempts at any sort of Sanitation. Whilst had in some of the French troops were seen using the garden and courtyard for purposes of nature, spaces for cooking purposes had been well burnt out by having a good layer of straw. All personnel accommodated on 1st floor, one head British on head Indian Sector Call operating on M.O.S. gone on ground floor. Opened to receive wounded at 5est not to collect for MANCHESTER cas post. aid. | |

Army Form C. 2118.

Page 24.

# WAR DIARY
## or
## INTELLIGENCE SUMMARY.
(Erase heading not required.)

| Hour, Date, Place. | Summary of Events and Information. | Remarks and references to Appendices. |
|---|---|---|
| 1914 | | |
| Dec 12. BEUVRY | During the day collected Indian Sick from units billeted in neighbourhood | M.O/s Set A. ARRAS. |
| 13 " | at dusk sending out both ambulances & bearer personnel to MANCHESTER | |
| 14 " | Regt Aid Post to collect Sick & wounded. O.C. visited aid post & (12") | |
| 15 " | | |
| 16 BETHUNE | 2.0 to 3.30 PM on march. Billeted in Seminary at BETHUNE & shared accommodation with No 7 R.F.A. This Building makes a most excellent hospital, unlimited room, electric light & hot water, heating apparatus. | |
| 17 " | Major MELHUISH detained for leave. | |
| 18 " | Both ambulances sent to junctions on BEUVRY – CUINCHY road at 5.30 PM. Have ambulances & bearer company (under Lt WALSH) deployed to O.C. No 8. R.F.A BEUVRY at 10.30 PM as was Reptd in Meerut at rest billets. 17 wounded and 13 sick (Indian) during the day. | |
| 19 " | Major MELHUISH with bearers & 2 motor ambulances collected from and posts at GIVENCHY via the BEUVRY–CUINCHY front (across the La Bassée Canal), the Aux both ambulances with Bearers ad Juncts from the junctions on Hers road to BETHUNE, being to the distance (approx) some miles there and back) the horse ambulances Coel + H Leave done this Saturdays. 46 wounded 92 sick evact to A.S. |

Army Form C. 2118.

# WAR DIARY
## or
## INTELLIGENCE SUMMARY.

*(Erase heading not required.)*

Instructions regarding War Diaries and Intelligence Summaries are contained in F. S. Regs., Part II, and the Staff Manual respectively. Title pages will be prepared in manuscript.

| Hour, Date, Place. | Summary of Events and Information. | Remarks and references to Appendices |
|---|---|---|
| 1914 | | |
| Dec 20 BETHUNE | Major ODLUM collecting wrote Same arrangers as yesterday. The Officer informed that the cases over the canal was under the enemy's fire at all times. 126 wounded & 38 sick admitted at 142 evacuated by Red Cross Motor Convoy during the 24 hours. The average in hospital during the day was 150 approximately. | |
| Dec 21. BETHUNE | Captain BOYD proceeded at 2.45 P.M. with Bearer Co, two ambulances and Horse ambulances to collect wounded S of the La Bassée Canal in the triangle formed by the Canal & the BEUVRY — QUINCHY Road. 45 wounded & 13 sick admitted during the 24 hrs. 158 evacuated by the Red + Cnvoy away in hospital during the 24 hrs 155. | |
| Dec 22  " | Captain BOYD returns at 0.30am, at dusk Lt WALSH proceeded with two motor ambulances & personnel to form a dressing station at GORRE. he lit a Station manned by a British ambulance demand the night & gave assistance. During the night the dying down Cases were put on to an ambulance train at the BETHUNE STATION at the setting up Cases Achern | two/o SET A ARRAS. |

Army Form C. 2118.

Page 26.

# WAR DIARY
## or
## INTELLIGENCE SUMMARY.

(Erase heading not required.)

Instructions regarding War Diaries and Intelligence Summaries are contained in F. S. Regs., Part II, and the Staff Manual respectively. Title pages will be prepared in manuscript.

| Hour, Date, Place. | Summary of Events and Information. | Remarks and references to Appendices |
|---|---|---|
| 1914 | | |
| Dec 22. BETHUNE | — By the Red + made convoy to the clearing Hospital. The average in Hospital up to this time was 150 afternoon daily. | |
| 23. RAIMBERT | Left BETHUNE at 1.10 PM & got into billets at RAIMBERT at 7.30PM. Map Set A ARRAS. The delay being due to difficulty in obtaining billets. 40 cases of sivalli first admitted just before starts, were bought along. Ambulance closed. Two motor ambulances collecting sick from the Divn | Map Set A ARRAS. |
| 24 " | & transferred to No 6 B.F.A. at No 111 I.F.A. | |
| 25 to 31. | Ditto. During the week the weather was mild with showers at intervals during the day. There was a slight frost on 25th for a few hours. Total wounded since commencement of operations 896 } Total 524 } 1420. sick | |
| General Notes | (1) The Staff personnel worked well as there was no serious crime. The health of the Indian troops was remarkably good. The Rations | Appendices 283. |
| (F.S. Regs Part II 140 (I.ii.) | and clothing were good & ample. Those who showed any symptoms meant were ordered to their homes & set in to the A.D.M.S. | |
| | (2) The System of dealing with wounded is described in a letter to the A.D.M.S a copy of which is attached | |
| | (3) Equipment. After mobilisation at ... the carriage of military ... | Appendix 4. |

Army Form C. 2118.

Pay 27.

# WAR DIARY
## or
## INTELLIGENCE SUMMARY.
*(Erase heading not required.)*

Instructions regarding War Diaries and Intelligence Summaries are contained in F. S. Regs., Part II, and the Staff Manual respectively. Title pages will be prepared in manuscript.

| Hour, Date, Place. | Summary of Events and Information. | Remarks and references to Appendices |
|---|---|---|
| 1914<br>General Notes<br>(Continued) | (3) text books was felt. These might be kept up or part of the equipment of medical units with advantage.<br><br>(4) Lamps. These are very poor, the Ford's lamps do not give a satisfactory light for operative purposes, the Bull's eye lanters are useless. An acetylene outfit was purchased from the Imperial Light Co, 123 Victoria St. S.W. (Imperial F.Amb. outfit) for operating at sea, given every satisfaction. Electric flash lamps were obtained from J.H.Steward Ltd, 406 Strand W. and W.O. in lieu of the Bull's eye lanters as these are proving to be of greater value. These were purchased from the allotment made from the IMPERIAL INDIAN RELIEF FUND.<br><br>(5) Some special items were purchased for the same fund, they should be part of the standard equipment. Also additional syringes.<br><br>(6) Ambulance Transport. The horse ambulances are very slow & only suitable for short distances, see note under Jan 26, this point will easily have been performed in an hour with motor ambulances. M.S. | |

Army Form C. 2118.

Pg 28.

# WAR DIARY
## or
## INTELLIGENCE SUMMARY.

*(Erase heading not required.)*

Instructions regarding War Diaries and Intelligence Summaries are contained in F. S. Regs., Part II, and the Staff Manual respectively. Title pages will be prepared in manuscript.

| Hour, Date, Place. | Summary of Events and Information. | Remarks and references to Appendices |
|---|---|---|
| General Notes (Continued) | (6) Also see note under Dec 19, as examples. The Red Cross motor convoys have evacuated cases down to the clearing hospitals & kept the circuit clear, most expediting and successfully all through. Jan 1. 1915 [signature] O.C. 112 FA | |

Appendix 1.

Copy of Telegram 618/29. Dated 6.8.14

From ADMS 3rd DIVN   To   O.C. Lahore Cantonment

Please direct Major BROWSE to report himself to D.A.D.M.S for command of No 112 I.F.A.

---

Appendix 2.  Copy of letter O.C. 20 dated 22.11.1914. from O.C. 112 I.F.A

To A.D.M.S Lahore Divn I.E.Force

In accordance with your 445 of 20.11.1914 I herewith submit the names of the two following men

1. 2nd class Senior Sub Assistant Surgeon GAURI SHANKAR.
On October 24 at LAVENTIE he tended the Indian wounded under shell fire & his conduct was specially noted by Major J.M. SLOAN DSO RAMC & Major A.W. GIBSON RAMC who were present at the time.

2. 1st class Sub Assistant Surgeon NARAYAN-PARSHAD SUKUL No 997 — He has shown great energy and ability and has been untiring in his devotion to duty. I consider his work to have been of an exceptionally valuable nature.

---

Appendix 3.  Copy of a letter Confidential No 1 from O.C. 112 I.F.A. 8.12.1914

To A.D.M.S Lahore Divn I.E.Force

Reference your Confidential No 2 of date

All the Officers of this unit serving under me have done most excellent and steady work, although I am unable to say that any one in particular has shown zeal or ability in excess of his brother Officers

Appendix 3. (Continued)

Major H.M. MELHUISH commanded the unit in my absence during an exceptional push of work, when he was very short handed, & his work has no doubt been noted by you.

As regards other ranks No 997 1st class Sub Assistant Surgeon NARAYAN-PARSHAD SUKUL has in my opinion shown exceptional ability and merit all though, as reported in my No O.C. 20 of 22.11.1914 & I consider he is well deserving of mention

Appendix 4. Memo to A.D.M.S. Yelu Div B.52 - 26.12.1914
(with reference to Surgical procedure adopted by unit.)

A permanent staff consisting of a Sub Assistant Surgeon & menial establishment is detailed for the operation and dressing rooms. This staff is excused all other duty when the unit is open for the reception of wounded.

Each man is asked when brought into the room 1. Who dressed the wound 2. When it was dressed and if iodine was used.

If the wound has been dressed by an M.O. during the last 12 or 18 hours & there is no soaking of blood though the dressings & the latter are clean and dry, nothing further is done & the man is passed on into the ward.

If the dressing has been applied by a comrade or other unqualified person & is soaked through with blood or looks generally unsatisfactory, it is removed with the usual aseptic precautions by an Officer. Tincture of Iodine is freely used over it (unless the open surface is so large as to contraindicate it's use over the whole surface). If there is a very large gaping wound a few sutures are sometimes applied, but never so as to close a wound completely or interfere with absolutely free drainage. Haemorrhage is stopped, necessary splints &c applied & the wound dressed with sterilised antiseptic gauze (The affected limb or surrounding part of body is well washed.)

Antitetanic serum was at first given in special cases and in small doses as there was a limited quantity & only a small hypodermic syringe with which to inject it.

P.T.O.

Appendix 4 (Continued)

— ATS is now given to all cases under strict aseptic precautions in 1500 unit doses (except when there is such a large number of cases as to absolutely preclude its use, all Parades, or serious wounds are injected under such circumstances).

Notes as to procedure adopted are made on the Transfer Return with which each man is provided.

Jan 1. 1915

A.T. Byatt
Major RAMC
O.C. 112 F.A.

# WAR DIARY

## of 112. Indian Field Ambulance Lahore Division.

### From 1st January 1915 To 31st January 1915

121/44/01
Jan. 1915

**Army Form C. 2118.**

# WAR DIARY
## *or*
## INTELLIGENCE SUMMARY.

(*Erase heading not required.*)

No 3 Section
A. G's Office at Base
I.E. Force
Passed to _____ S. Sect<sup>n</sup>
on 7-2-15

*Instructions regarding War Diaries and Intelligence Summaries are contained in F. S. Regs., Part II, and the Staff Manual respectively. Title pages will be prepared in manuscript.*

ADJUTANT GENERAL INDIA
184 WD
-7. FEB. 1915
BASE OFFICE

Pages 1 to 7.

| Hour, Date, Place. | Summary of Events and Information. | Remarks and references to Appendices |
|---|---|---|
| | 112 Indian<br><br>FIELD AMBULANCE<br><br>LAHORE DIVISION<br><br>I.E.F.<br><br>Jan<sup>y</sup> 1<sup>st</sup> to 31<sup>st</sup>. 1915. | |

Army Form C. 2118.

112 I.F.A.
1915.
Page 1.

# WAR DIARY
or
# INTELLIGENCE SUMMARY.

(Erase heading not required.)

Instructions regarding War Diaries and Intelligence Summaries are contained in F. S. Regs., Part II, and the Staff Manual respectively. Title pages will be prepared in manuscript.

| Hour, Date, Place. | Summary of Events and Information. | Remarks and references to Appendices |
|---|---|---|
| 1915 | | |
| January 1st REMBERT to 5th | Unit ordered to remain in constant readiness for immediate move until further orders. | |
| 6th " | Major ODLUM proceeded on 7 days leave | |
| 7th " | Captain BOYD ditto | |
| 8th–12th " | Getting to note. Weather variable. Heavy showers & storms with fine intervals. Major BROWSE returned from 7 days leave | |
| 13th " | Received message 15 (Appendix 1) from A.D.M.S. at 4.30 P.M. Wrote to the SIRHIND Bde. suggesting BURBURE – CHOCQUES – BETHUNE route which was agreed to (Ref. maps 932 B.C.) | Appendix 1. map BELGIUM 1/100,000 5.a. |
| 14th VIELLE CHAPELLE | Sent interpreter at 8.30 A.M. to see the state of road between BURBURE and ALLOUAGNE as noted dubtful in map. Reports good so left at 11.0 A.M. Reached BETHUNE 2.30 P.M. Water over at 1/2 feed. As not needed High LOCON I reported to A.D.M.S. 2nd Division who had no orders to give at told me to carry on according to instructions already received. Lt WALSH at the Interpreter met in ahead to see about billets. Reached VIELLE CHAPELLE at 5.30 P.M. Billets suitable for a getting ambulance. Arranged packed Round Church, Horses in open. | |
| 15th LACOUTURE | No billet at VIELLE CHAPELLE suitable for a ward, being occupied by Ammn. Battery, only other suitable building occupied by B section of No 5 F.F.A. | |

# WAR DIARY
## or
## INTELLIGENCE SUMMARY.

*(Erase heading not required.)*

Army Form C. 2118.

Page 2

| Hour, Date, Place. | Summary of Events and Information. | Remarks and references to Appendices |
|---|---|---|
| 1915<br>Jany 15th LACOUTURE | Saw the ADMS 2nd Division who had no orders to give & informed me he was not under his orders. During the forenoon an Officer of No 113 I.F.A came in and said his unit was on the way with orders to billet in VIEILLE CHAPELLE. Under these circumstances I saw the G.O.C Sirhind Bde who was in the village & asked for instructions. He suggested the unit opening up at RICHEBOURG ST VAAST but on its being pointed out that the place being close behind the trenches was not suited for an advanced dressing station, He instructed me to proceed to LACOUTURE, obtain billets and open up. This I did at 2.30 PM. On 3.30 PM accompanied by Major MELHUISH I visited the Brigade Head Quarters at RICHEBOURG ST VAAST & selected a Billet suitable for an advanced dressing station & arranged with the Brigade Major that a Sub Assist Surgeon, wd orderly, 25 bearers with the necessary equipment should remain here with two horse ambulances, a B.O. to sleep at the station at night to visit the aid posts in the early morning the road being considered safer during the day. — at 7.55 PM I received a memo from Lt Colonel Wray Sm.O Sirhind & Jullundur Bdes who had arrived at VIEILLE CHAPELLE ordering me there to bed arranged that No 5 E.F.A should collect all the Indian Sick & wounded during the night and ...<br>A.B.S | with BELGIUM 100,000<br>5. a |

# WAR DIARY
## or
## INTELLIGENCE SUMMARY.
*(Erase heading not required.)*

Army Form C. 2118.

Page 3.

| Hour, Date, Place. | Summary of Events and Information. | Remarks and references to Appendices |
|---|---|---|
| **1915** Jan 15th LACOUTURE | ordered me to set a S.A.S. as interpreter to the advanced dressing station of No 5. This was done at the B^tte begin informed of the change in plans. | map BELGIUM 100,000 5.a |
| " 16th ZELOBES | Visited S.M.O R^les at VIELLE CHAPELLE 9.0 AM & arranged to accompany him to see G.O.C. Sirhind B^de at 11.0 AM. On my return to billet found 2 officers sent in advance from Jullundur B^de with orders to take over the billets in which the Ambulance was open. Under these circumstances I ordered the Hospital to close and stood by ready to move out. On my way to VIELLE CHAPELLE to proceed to ZELOBES, as soon as billets at 11.15 AM who ordered me to proceed to ZELOBES at once at this place I found 2 sectn of No 7 B.F.A. at my own tent. On arrival at this place I met the A.D.M.S LAHORE DIV whom I accompanied in a search for billets. We found nothing suitable as a word except the big Cry convent the S^me which was used for No 7 B.F.A. when evacuated by the Sectn of No 5 E.F.A. who up to this time had received no orders to evacuate. Received orders from A.D.M.S to bring my unit to ZELOBES at noon between ap. at 1.30 PM (aft/hr) I returned to LACOUTURE at on my way met the G.O.C. Jullundur B^de who was seeing troops in. I asked him when it would be safe for me to have by at back & was informed probably in about an hours time, on reaching LACOUTURE I found the | |

Army Form C. 2118.

# WAR DIARY
## or
## INTELLIGENCE SUMMARY.
(Erase heading not required.)

Page 4.

Instructions regarding War Diaries and Intelligence Summaries are contained in F. S. Regs., Part II, and the Staff Manual respectively. Title pages will be prepared in manuscript.

| Hour, Date, Place. | Summary of Events and Information. | Remarks and references to Appendices |
|---|---|---|
| January 16. ZELOBES 1915 | Ambulance ready to move at once. After Gan Officer to the Jullundur Bde. Hdrs. their transport was ordered to move to some delay on the road. Several Rolls of troops came in at some carts and motor lorries at 3:30 P.M. as usual, were sent to the lines. I asked at the Bde. Head Quarters whether it would now be safe for me to move back as I was told it would be advisable for me to do so. I set out & despatched an Officer along the road to see if all clear down to ZELOBES & on his return that all was clear I marched off & at 3.50 P.M. on reaching a point half way between VIEILLE CHAPELLE and ZELOBES I came on to some of the Jullundur Bde. carts stuck in the mud on the side of the road. I pulled my transport into the mud on by side as being busy light it would more easily be moved than the heavily loaded wagons in the brigade convoy. However in passing by ambulances two more brigade wagons got bogged owing to their heavy loads and not very skilful driving. To add to the difficulty 2 Sections of No 7 R.F.A came up behind & completely blocked me in rear & several cars came up behind the Brigade convoy. Men was set to | Map BELGIUM 1/100,000 5a |

Army Form C. 2118.

Page 5

# WAR DIARY
## or
## INTELLIGENCE SUMMARY.

(Erase heading not required.)

Instructions regarding War Diaries and Intelligence Summaries are contained in F. S. Regs., Part II, and the Staff Manual respectively. Title pages will be prepared in manuscript.

1915

| Hour, Date, Place. | Summary of Events and Information. | Remarks and references to Appendices |
|---|---|---|
| Jan 16. ZELOBES | dark I set off to stop here traffic at each end & road as as it was getting along the road. I then looked up being carts which were in rear up a side lane as the lorren convoy were set to work unloading a bullock cart wagons which were stuck. The post was extremely closed at 8.0 P.M. Major ODLUM did apparently good work as the leaves all worked with the greatest energy. I left 4 lorry wagons on the Side road for the night as it was very dark & the lines blocked. | Map BELGIUM 1/100,000 5.a. |
| Jan 17th. PARADIS | At 7.0 AM arranged by Major ODLUM I was up at daybreak in the wagons left out. At 8:30 AM a Staff Officer arrived at the billet (ZELOBES) & advised me to get 4b to my destination as soon as possible. made at 9:30 AM & when on side road set on 2 lorries before entering Oud Sactin, one to prevent cd. and a stop all traffic from entering at the other & return & report to Front Officer. Reached PARADIS at 11.0 AM and found excellent billets. A.B.C's in good outbuildings of the farm at the + Troops to S.D. Church. — A.S.C. drivers & Boys slept at Sub Officer Surg in Girls' School. All Officers under men in various Billets in Village | |

Gulab Singh & Sons, Calcutta—No. 22 Army C.—5-8-14—1,07,000.

Army Form C. 2118.

Page 6.

# WAR DIARY
or
# INTELLIGENCE SUMMARY.
(Erase heading not required.)

Instructions regarding War Diaries and Intelligence Summaries are contained in F. S. Regs., Part II, and the Staff Manual respectively. Title pages will be prepared in manuscript.

| Hour, Date, Place. | Summary of Events and Information. | Remarks and references to Appendices |
|---|---|---|
| 1915 | | |
| Jan'y 17th PARADIS | Capt. BOYD joined 113 LFA as a temporary measure. | |
| 18th " | Sunny all day with practice theme. Lt. WALSH left at 11.0 p.m. to join the 59th Rifles FF India on urgent orders from ADMS Lahore Div. | |
| 19th " | Dull & overcast, steady thaw. Water rising at 5.0 p.m. over most of the road between the 2 fords to St Omer & the girls school. | |
| 20th " | Dull & overcast, water at same level. | |
| 21st " | Rain all day, flood rose some inches during the day. Major ODLUM joined the 15th Sikhs on duty under urgent orders from ADMS. | |
| 22nd RAMBERT | Left PARADIS at 8.30 AM in to a wagon after rugged owing to difficulty of obtaining good plug to float a dally of 3 lorries deceased in 1st mile. Arrived at farm billet at 5.30 PM. Brigade Billets in Brewmue occupied by 125th Rifles so obtained a suitable one at the school of St Pierre. | |
| 23 " | Rect. Two days pub/news to meet | |
| 24-25- " | Order to be in state of readiness preparedness at 10.15 Jany [?] from Major [?] BOYD detailed for 1st 113 LFA. | |
| 26-27 " | Paraded the junior at 2 am notice. 26. Rain — Hard frost. | |
| 28 " | Had visit of B.G. for Sam. Surg General [?] Leatheson C.I.G. paid an unofficial visit to unit in afternoon. | W[?] |
| 29 — | | |

Army Form C. 2118.

Pg 7.

# WAR DIARY
## or
## INTELLIGENCE SUMMARY.

(Erase heading not required.)

Instructions regarding War Diaries and Intelligence Summaries are contained in F. S. Regs., Part II, and the Staff Manual respectively. Title pages will be prepared in manuscript.

| Hour, Date, Place. | Summary of Events and Information. | Remarks and references to Appendices |
|---|---|---|
| 1915<br>Jan 30. RAIMBERT<br>" 31st -<br>LOZINGHEM | Routine work. Three. Lt ANDERSON & Lt KENNEDY joined as a fatiguing horsemen from III I.F.A.<br><br>Left RAIMBERT at 9am. and LOZINGHEM at 1.15 P.m at Arrive in billets vacated by III I.F.A. at 84 Sick left by them. During the afternoon the 2 mule ambulances also taken over from III collected 53 cases. All they were evacuated by 9.0.7 mule convoy to LILLERS that evening. Chiefly cases Pyrexia & Respiratory troubles. Lt KENNEDY was placed on the Sick list & sent to the Divis. Receiving at LILLERS | C.S. Byrath Majors<br>OC. III I.F.A<br>Indian Div. I.E.F. |

Serial No. 154

121/4/9

# WAR DIARY

**112 Indian Field Ambulance, Lahore Division.**

From 1st February 1915 to 28th February 1915.

121/4/9
Feb. 1915

# WAR DIARY
## or
## INTELLIGENCE SUMMARY.

*(Erase heading not required.)*

Army Form C. 2118.

Page 6.

| Hour, Date, Place. | Summary of Events and Information. | Remarks and references to Appendices |
|---|---|---|
| CALONNE. Feb 1st 1915 | Unit marched from LOZINGHEM to CALONNE 8.0 AM to 2.0 PM. Collected 59 men during the march, chiefly chest complaints. A good Billet. Hospital in school, A.B.C. 3 sections in Barn, D Section on shed at side of School yard. Orders to be ready to move at two hours notice. | Map FRANCE 1:40,000 (Bethune) |
| Feb 2nd | Capt ANDERSON I.M.S. proceeded to 113 I.F.A. Hospital, but collecting Sick & Wounded as usual. [JULLUNDUR Bde] | |
| 3rd | | |
| 4th | Capt ANDERSON I.M.S. rejoined from 113 I.F.A. Duties as usual. | |
| 5th, 6th | | |
| 7th | Major DOLOM I.M.S. rejoined from 15 Sikhs. | |
| 8th | Duties as usual. | |
| 9th | | |
| 10th | Capt ANDERSON placed on Sick List with Laryngitis & transferred to Clearing Stn. | |
| LOCON 10th | Marched to LOCON in rear of Brigade Transport, Roads bad as some of the transport in front got bogged passing a motor Lorry causing a delay of some two hours. Billet in LOCON Écis. Prohibited from going in the School Square X 7 a q-2 at the personal in Vehicle Buildings on the same road between the School & Canal bridge. | |
| " 11th | Collecting Sick only, from Corps passing. | |

Army Form C. 2118.

Page 9.

# WAR DIARY
## or
## INTELLIGENCE SUMMARY.

*(Erase heading not required.)*

Instructions regarding War Diaries and Intelligence Summaries are contained in F. S. Regs., Part II, and the Staff Manual respectively. Title pages will be prepared in manuscript.

| Hour, Date, Place. | Summary of Events and Information. | Remarks and references to Appendices |
|---|---|---|
| 1915 | | |
| LOCON Feb. 12 to 22. | Received Orders to collecting Sick from troops in favour of Divisional units moving to rest. | |
| CALONNE 23rd 24th | Marched from LOCON 8.30 AM to arrive in same billets as before. Collecting Sick from JULLUNDUR Bde. Major ODLUM placed on Sick Rep. wine Sciatica. | |
| " 25-26-27 28. | moved to Bde rest. Lieut WALSH returned from Army duty with 59th Rifles F.F. Captain BOYD left for Army duty, Beatles & discharges of clothes & troops. | |
| (General Notes) | The weather was cold Showery & changeable during the month. There was 15 days on which (considerable) rain fell. On 22nd, 24th – 26th there was heavy heavy frost at night but thaw during the day. 337 admissions during the month. Regimental divisions account for 72 front trenches 142 & fever NYD 54 | |

B Boyle
Major L
O.C. 111 FA

# WAR DIARY
### with Appendices.
## OF
## 112 Indian Field Ambulance, Lahore Division.

From 1st March 1915 to 31st March 1915

Army Form C. 2118.

# WAR DIARY
## or
## INTELLIGENCE SUMMARY.

*(Erase heading not required.)*

112 Indian
FIELD AMBULANCE
LAHORE DIVISION
I.E.F.

March 1st to 31st 1915.

Pages 10 — 14

-5. APR 1915
ADJUTANT GENERAL INDIA
BASE OFFICE

| Hour, Date, Place. | Summary of Events and Information. | Remarks and references to Appendices |
|---|---|---|

# WAR DIARY or INTELLIGENCE SUMMARY

Army Form C. 2118.

Page 10

| Hour, Date, Place. | Summary of Events and Information. | Remarks and references to Appendices |
|---|---|---|
| MARCH 1st–4th CALONNE | Collecting Sec from the JULLUNDUR Bde. Nothing of note. | |
| 5th " | Lieut W.C. PATON IMS joined the unit | |
| 6th " | Instruction sent to ADMS that the Army Bearer Corps men refuse to make any family allotments, all are willing to make fin-allowances by hundi order. Only one allowance has been made for the OCB two months to persuade them. Various excuses are made. | |
| 7th " | Collecting Sec to 15th Sikhs – 59th Rifles, 3rd Sqn. | |
| 8th " | In addition to above collecting sec from 9th Bhopal I. and 129th Baluchis. | Appendix 1. |
| 9th " | Attached to FEROZEPORE Bde. ADMS Lieut 78 | Copy of ADMS War Diary 9.3.15 |
| 10th " | Collecting Sec for Brigade as other units before Cable left the area. | |
| 11th " | The Brigade marched out at 6.0 P.M. Ambulance remained quietly to move under orders of ADMS the unit marched at 6.30 AM to billets at Sy R.31.C. all in by 8.30 AM. About 9.45 the 9th Gurkha Rifles marched in having been ordered after severe days in the trenches, they had been allotted the same billets. Under the circumstances I saw the G.O.C. Dera Doon Bn to which the unit belonged and suggested that the closed ambulance as it was only within a quick fresh should vacate the billets to enable the regiment to get a rest. The G.O.C. agreed & at 11.0 AM the billets were occupied by the Battalion. Lieut WALSH proceeded to CALONNE to get orders from the ADMS who instructed me to find other billets. Whilst doing so the Dera Doon Bn received order to return home, so at this unit re-occupied the original billets at 6.30 P.M. | Map FRANCE (BETHUNE) 1/40,000 |
| 12th " | | |

Army Form C. 2118.

Page 11.

# WAR DIARY
or
## INTELLIGENCE SUMMARY.
(Erase heading not required.)

Instructions regarding War Diaries and Intelligence Summaries are contained in F. S. Regs., Part II, and the Staff Manual respectively. Title pages will be prepared in manuscript.

| Hour, Date, Place. | Summary of Events and Information. | Remarks and references to Appendices |
|---|---|---|
| March 13. ZELOBES 1915 | Arrived from our Billets at 9.0 A.M. and the run from 128 I.F.A. Hospital in a two strand of January Sq R 27 & C 1/6 a good Building opposite the end of the VIELLE CHAPELLE Road. Trying down cases, operating and dressing on the ground floor, all cases able to get up the stairs go up to upper room. 25 cases and be accommodated (lying down stretcher cases) in the lower room and 12.5 upstairs. This number of cases were extremely in the Building before the huts convoy cleared the unit at midnight of 13-14th. At 12.15 (noon) Major MELMUISH & Lt WALSH with S.A.S. GAURI SHANKAR and ALI JAN & 11 Bearer company proceeded to Sq S 8 a 9/5 to form an advanced dressing station, relieving 9107 B.F.A. They placed to act to collect wounded in connection with the Lahore division & other units for aid posts in front of the position at NEUVE CHAPELLE. This collecting was done in the evening and early morning as being the night when necessary. | Map FRANCE (BETHUNE) 1/40.000 |
| 14th | 94 wounded 119 Sick power through the ambulance | |
| 15th | 91 wounded 54 Sick ditto | No change |
| 16th | 02 wounded 9 Sick ditto | No change |
| | 13 wounded 54 Sick | No change |
| | Lieut PATON with S.A.S. SUDAMA RAM & went forward relieved the Bearer company at the advanced dressing Station. On arrival came orders from the A.D.M.S. the names of Major HARMELHUISH – S.A.S. GAURI SHANKAR at the S.A.S. NARAYAN PARSHAD SURIN – have sent in for good work during period 10 to the | Appendix 2. Copy of letter O.C. 57 F.A.315 to ADMS |

Army Form C. 2118.

Page 12

# WAR DIARY
## or
## INTELLIGENCE SUMMARY.
(Erase heading not required.)

| Hour, Date, Place. 1915 | Summary of Events and Information. | Remarks and references to Appendices |
|---|---|---|
| March 17. ZELOBES | At abt 9.45 AM the enemy's explosive shells burst in the advanced dressing station, practically demolish the Building. The following men of this unit were killed Sepy (no 1 Orderly) ZAMAN KHAN (130 Baluchis) He was attending the sick at the time. No 4163 Bearer PITAMBER of this unit was dangerously wounded. The following sick men were killed<br>1707 Naraha HARI CHAND 1/1 G.R. 4669 4/4 R RAM BAHADUR GARTI 1/4 G.R.<br>3053 Rifleman HAST BIR ''<br>393 '' MAN BIR ''<br>attached to Lieut PATON's report Appendix B.<br>This Officer offers to Brave acted with coolness & bravery, the conduct of the bearer also deserves Praise. They were steady at work under heavy circumstances. The names of the Serais were 4009 Naik WADHAWA was forwards to the ADMS.<br>The Bearer coys. was at once withdrawn by the ADMS. In the evening I visited the firginated aid posts with Capt. Lees SLOAN D.S.O. in lieu MELHUISH & collected the sick & wounded, ambulances were left down the night at the corner S 2 C 2/2 et a Sub Assist Surgeon Jemave with 8 Stretchers at a central aid post and collected sick & wounded at dawn, he came in to his quarter after this. All was quiet during the night. | Appendix B. letter of 53. 19.3.15 fr O.C. 112 IFA to ADMS forwar pkt of Lieut PATON in the Bath of advanced dressing station on 17.3.15.<br>X<br>Bearer PITAMBER 4163<br>died in LUCKNOW clearing station on March 17th. |
| March 18 " | On arrival wird a telegram from O.C. 129 Baluchis two Brs ambulances | |

# WAR DIARY
## or
## INTELLIGENCE SUMMARY.
*(Erase heading not required.)*

Army Form C. 2118.

Page 13.

| Hour, Date, Place. | Summary of Events and Information. | Remarks and references to Appendices |
|---|---|---|
| 1915 | | |
| March 18. ZELOBES | Were sent over to evacuate some wounded from the Bayonets and post at this point by decease of his unit. S.A.S. SUDAN Ram in charge stopped that some shells fell close to the convoy when returning. A/Surg. RICHEBAR i/c G B.F.A sent up the Officers & Nursing personnel with wagons for the night but Bright Collection. | |
| 19th " | Stood half hour up with the horses empty of wagons. Ready of route. | |
| 20th " | No. G B.F.A arrived for this but we might (illeg.) if wanted & sick for and from | |
| 21st " | Captain Boyd went up with the horses empty in wagons. Ready of route. | |
| 22nd - ROBECQ | The ambulance closed at Zecamhd to ROBECQ on relief by 130 I.F.A. The totals of Sick & wounded admitted to the unit during the spell of work at the front between March 13 & 21st was  WOUNDED 222 | |
| 23 - 24 " " | Ambulance Closed. Readmin with sick. SICK  359. Been completely - ready of road. | |
| 25th " | ditto | with Captain BOYD leapt for temporary duty, Butler of Hospital temps. |
| 26th " | ditto | All have mules with light no 7 days |
| | Orders at Ords weekly of personnel handed over to made roles at to G.S. Wagon | |

Army Form C. 2118.

# WAR DIARY
## *or*
## INTELLIGENCE SUMMARY.
*(Erase heading not required.)*

Page 14.

| Hour, Date, Place | Summary of Events and Information | Remarks and references to Appendices |
|---|---|---|
| March 27 ROBECQ 1915 | Ambulance closed. General fracture ward, Medical & field work & Sub Assist Surgeons & Census Continuing. | |
| 28-29 | Ditto | |
| 30 | Ditto S/A WALSH proceeded to the Divisional Train for temp. duty. | |
| | Weather: 1st week cold & dull, (Mar), heavy showers with high wind. 2nd week dull with occasional showers, slightly warmer. 3rd week warm, some bright days & warm showers. 4th week bright & genial, heavy frost 27th, 28th & 29th mng. Cold front all day — Shade. | |

O.C. Bird
O.C. 111 I.F.A.

Appendix 1.  WAR DIARY  112 I.F.A.

Copy of A.D.M.S. LAHORE Divn wire 78. 9.3.15.

Reference para seven of operation orders No 66 dated 6th March by G.O.C. Lahore Division the medical units allotted to your brigade are No 112 I.F.A. and two sections of No 7 B.F.A. at present in CALONNE aaa Major BROWSE IMS. will act as S.M.O. of Brigade aaa Address FEROZEPORE 15FB a copy to Field Ambulances concerned.

Appdix 1.

Appendix 2.   WAR DIARY 112 I.F.A.

Copy of letter OC 51 from OC 112 IFA. TO ADMS LAHORE D/v

Reference yours 13 of 16.3.15

I wish to bring to your notice the name of Major H.M. MELHUISH IMS who was in command of the bearer Company at RICHEBOURG, also 1st class Senior S.A.S GAURI SHANKAR who was in sub charge.

The wounded were collected and sent in most expeditiously, with dressings etc applied in a very thorough manner. The dressing station was under shell fire frequently during this time.

I also wish to bring to your notice the heroic and highly meritorious work done by 1st class Sub Assistant Surgeon NARAYAN PARSHAD SUKUL, his assistance and work have been invaluable to me both in the period under mention and all through the war.

17.3.15.

G.D. Sprawson
Major
O.C. 112 I.F.A.

Appendix 2

Appendix 3.   WAR DIARY 112 I.F.A.

Letter O.C. 53 19.3.15 f— O.C. 112 I.F.A. to A.D.M.S.
LAHORE D'Vⁿ

I attach a report from Lieut PATON I.M.S. of the shelling of the advanced dressing station of this unit on March 17th.

All ranks seem to have acted with coolness and presence of mind and Lt PATON informs me that the men of the Army Bearer Corps were all cool and steady and behaved very well. No 4009 Naik WADHAWA deserves credit as the senior A.B.C. man present.

G. [signature]
Major [?]
O.C. 112 I.F.A.
19.3.15

Appendix 3

18.3.15.

To OC, 112 Indian Field Ambulance.

On the evening of 16.3.15 I with 2nd Class S.A.S. Sudama Ram and a party of 20 bearers relieved Lieut. Walsh and 20 bearers at the Advanced dressing station at Richebourg. About 5.30 p.m. Lieut. Biggam R.A.M.C. of No. 8 B.F.A. advanced dressing station and I with a party of our bearers went to the aid posts and collected a number of wounded, and later in the night I sent up bearer parties for some more wounded. These were all evacuated about 11.30 p.m.

During that evening & night

a fair number of shells fell into the village of Richebourg and some went over our heads but none fell very near. On the following morning, 17.3.15, about 8.30 a.m. Lieut. Biggam R.A.M.C., Lieut. Stratford R.A.M.C. and I with a party of bearers from No 8. B.F.A. collected a few wounded from the aid posts. On our way back on the road from Windy Corner towards Richebourg 3 high explosive shells fell into the field about 30 yds. behind us, but did no harm. About 9.45 when I was having breakfast in No. 8. B.F.A. dressing station (about 50 yds from our dressing station) we heard a shell burst very near, and Lieut. Stratford looked out to see where it had gone, & said it had hit our dressing station. Lieut. Stratford, Lieut. Biggam & I ran along. We found that a shell had come in through the roof. One or two men were seen to be dead and two severely wounded. While Lieut Stratford and I were lifting out one wounded man through the back door, and Lieut. Biggam was coming in at the front door, another shell hit the next room. We got the two wounded men out to the back and the other men who had been hit were seen to be dead. Two Stretcher and some bearers were got, and the two severely wounded men were carried on the stretchers (Lieut. Biggam & Lieut. Stratford going with them) round the left side of the house to some dug-outs in front. While they were going to the dug-outs a shrapnel shell burst and Capt. Dunbar, a gunner officer, was hit through the head by a shrapnel bullet, and subsequently died. Lieut. Biggam had his left hand grazed by a bit of the same shell. In the meantime I saw that there were no more men left in the house, and took the uninjured men to the shelter of some dug-outs of a battery, a short distance

37

to the right of our building, while we were going there, another shell burst just behind the house. After that for about an hour the shelling continued in the direction of Richebourg Church.

Immediately after the first shell hit the dressing station No. 4183 Bearer Pitambar entered the building to help in getting the wounded out, and No. 3376 Hav. Jabbar Khan and No. 3890 Ward orderly Sadar Din were just on the point of entering when the second shell struck the building. Bearer Pitambar was one of the two men who was severely wounded, both legs being fractured. 2nd Class S.A.S. Sudama Ram also rendered useful help in getting the men together and directing them to the dug outs.

aid in getting the stretcher bearers for the two wounded. After things quieted down I removed the dressing station to part of the building occupied by No. 8. B.F.A. and had the dead buried.
The casualties were :-

### Killed.

1767 Hav. Hari Chand    1/1 Gurkha Rifles
8053 Sep. Hast Bir      1/1 Gurkha R.
4869 L.Nk. Ran Bahadur Gharti 1/4 G.R.
3139 Ward orderly Zaman Khan
                        130" Baluchis.

### Died of wounds at the Dressing Station:-

393 Sep. Man Bir   1/1 Gurkha R.

Severely wounded & evacuated to 112 I.F.A.
4/83 Bearer Pitamber
(He subsequently died).

About 5.30 pm, under orders from the A.D.M.S., the dressing station was left and we returned to Zelobe.

Capt Dunbar, who was hit on the head by shrapnel, was attended to in the dug-out by Lieut Biggam, and died in about ½ hour.

W.C. Paton.
Lt. I.M.S.

121/5504

April 1915

121/5504

Serial No 154.

mss
F

# WAR DIARY
with appendices.

112 Indian Field Ambulance, Lahore Division

From 1st April 1915 To 30th April 1915

Army Form C. 2118.

Pg 15

# WAR DIARY
## or
## INTELLIGENCE SUMMARY.
(Erase heading not required.)

Instructions regarding War Diaries and Intelligence Summaries are contained in F.S. Regs., Part II. and the Staff Manual respectively. Title pages will be prepared in manuscript.

| Hour, Date, Place | Summary of Events and Information | Remarks and references to Appendices |
|---|---|---|
| April 1st ROBECQ 1915 | Ambulance closed by 2nd [illegible] Moving field work [illegible] etc | |
| 2nd | ditto. Knife rash & mud [illegible] [illegible] became for 7 days leave | |
| 3rd to 5th | " | |
| 6th | ditto | |
| 7th | ditto [illegible] [illegible] [illegible] No 7 gas [illegible] | |
| 8th | [illegible] sick [illegible] [illegible] [illegible] [illegible] [illegible] [illegible] [illegible] | |
| 9th | ditto — [illegible] [illegible] [illegible] | |
| 10th | The Ambulance passed by Sub. Dr. 15th [illegible] — Patients | |
| 11th | ditto (15 [illegible] only) [illegible] BROWSE [illegible] for [illegible] | |
| 12th | April 9th [illegible] [illegible] ordered to be after 11. | |
| 13th | | |
| 14th–15th | The DDMS IAC [illegible] the [illegible] at 3.15 from & inspected the No 10 | |
| 16th | [illegible] building used as [illegible] | |
| A 7th | Return as above. Holding tents & [illegible] [illegible]. SAS Brigade [illegible] | |
| 7 — 18 " | to the 4th (Guards) [illegible] under orders 6 Army 5 FC[illegible] | |
| | Lt. F.J. ANDERSON [illegible] the [illegible] for duty, [illegible] [illegible] | |
| 19 — 22 " | Quoting Duty [illegible] | |
| 23 " | Captain R. KELSALL [illegible] On arrival for duty. Lt. Anderson [illegible] | |
| | 111 IFA. | |

# WAR DIARY
## or
## INTELLIGENCE SUMMARY.
*(Erase heading not required.)*

Army Form C. 2118.

Page 16.

| Hour, Date, Place | Summary of Events and Information | Remarks and references to Appendices |
|---|---|---|
| April 24. | (under orders from ADMS - LAHORE DIVISION (Telegram 186) the unit left ROBECQ at 3.0 PM for KRUIX TRAELE and South of MT DES CATS via LE GRAND PACAUT - VERTE RUE - LA RUE DU BOIS - VIEUX BERQUIN - STRAZELE and FLETRE. Owing to the onwards army of traffic the unit did not reach the new place till 9.30 PM, owing to this being no one to ask the best route the most direct road on the map was chosen ie the second turning to the right after turning to the left along the main road from Hazebrouck the village (Here is said to be the Rue Vert ? of the Rue). At the first x-roads two officers who met climb'd went to proceed on to the next +. This was not recognized as the x-roads going E.S.W. of the main road was unmetalled and looked like farm roads, on reaching the vicinity where the point reached was recognized it was impossible to turn owing to the road being too narrow for the "cook" of the Q.S. waggons, it was therefore decided to proceed on and turn back through GODEWAERSVELDE but on getting to the outskirts of this village the road was being blocked by 113 1FA a Brigade of artillery and a column of horse lorries, it was daylight before the ADMS could be found owing to the darkness & heavy rain which the road was sh*t. Destination was not reached until 5.0 AM after being guided by the ADMS Servt. The unit to march at 10.40 AM | map BELGIUM $\frac{1}{100,000}$ 5a |
| Ap. 25. KRUYSTRAETE | Guide of the ADMS at GODEWAERSVELDE had informed about the | |

Army Form C. 2118.

Say 17.

# WAR DIARY
## or
## INTELLIGENCE SUMMARY.
(Erase heading not required.)

| Hour, Date, Place | Summary of Events and Information | Remarks and references to Appendices |
|---|---|---|

**April 25**

Men & drivers animals were very tired. Received orders to march at 1.0 P.M. to Hutments N.E. of ODERDOM. On arrival the point 1/4 mile beyond WESTOUTRE was held by the Divn Supp On. To get Billets. Say there was room, so reported to A.D.M.S. but eventually got suitable ones near HASKEN.

**April 26. VLAMERTINGHE**

Marched to VLAMERTINGHE by 9 a.m. No Billets available. Obtained 3 huts in the Camp to the South as picked available. Also Gundy to billet wounded. Majr MELHUISH & Capt WALSH proceeded to S. JEAN with the Water Carts & I w. found an advanced dressing station. Wounded commenced to arrive at 1.00 P.M. Two huts were adapted as operating rooms & as soon as the huts had their own Billet wards wounded other huts were opened up, the props in them and (covered) with blankets. We that's have also been served by No. 7 R.F.A. installed in this my 5 huts at 14 tents were filled with wounded. From tea to opening to midday on April 27 436 wounded were dealt with, all spare hospital customaries. As first evacuation from the drsg stationes was slow as only two motor ambulances were available but later on in the night 3 motor became available for Divisional Train, Cars, etc. The Base Ambulances did excellent work but owing to the distance, some 5 or 6 miles they were not of much assistance (they have to field to go direct to Poste 4 miles a clear thro' YPRES.

**April 27** "

# WAR DIARY or INTELLIGENCE SUMMARY

Army Form C. 2118.

| Hour, Date, Place | Summary of Events and Information | Remarks and references to Appendices |
|---|---|---|
| 6/11/17 VLAMERTINGHE | During the day the village was shelled at intervals with great inaccuracy and shrapnel, & as men actually pitted in the Camp were destroyed at once. Men & gas attacks were made by whole and individuals were unable to get to their sleep which was much at the time only — that day between 3.50 & 4.00 am not much in the Camp as only the Smaller Group. Red wished the ambulance To Evacuate bath. Kits buses were placed at his disposal in the afternoon and here available in between 50th & 4th Cas. It was difficult to adequately deal after such a large number of men but it's a [illegible] at [illegible] were extremely made & issued. Each bus was [illegible] a lot of when the total of 250 in the ambulance was [illegible] the Wounds of the [illegible] the bullets [at] any body [illegible] & the [illegible] was given. Two or three were [illegible] [illegible] ½ pt., Red was taken in to the A.S.D. & not in the [illegible] to be [illegible] to the officers & [illegible] when his duties were [illegible] & to [illegible] [illegible] at no [illegible] be too [illegible] [illegible] of [illegible], the [illegible] were [illegible] on to the ward, if dust [illegible] & [illegible], a [illegible] or [illegible] of [illegible] he was [illegible] of [illegible] officers with [illegible]. Down at 24 bus in 11 — 27 & 26 — 318 [illegible] [illegible] |  |

Army Form C. 2118.

# WAR DIARY
## or
## INTELLIGENCE SUMMARY.
*(Erase heading not required.)*

Instructions regarding War Diaries and Intelligence Summaries are contained in F. S. Regs., Part II. and the Staff Manual respectively. Title pages will be prepared in manuscript.

Sep 14

| Hour, Date, Place | Summary of Events and Information | Remarks and references to Appendices |
|---|---|---|
| April 28. VLAMERTINGHE | The Unit was issued with bathing by order of ADMS on all July have got exhausted. Unit was given Relieved as the Reg't A.D had just finished with 8.0 P.M. on the day. 109 W.O. & men dealt with in this period. Thru in clear a total of 863 cases. TOTAL 967. In addition 104 Sick men dealt with. Shelly on leave. The village has been shelled at intervals. The unit marched to BELLS (betw. OUDERDOM & ….. ) then to hujd RENINGHELST as ground closed | |
| April 29. 30 | Attached is the report of hujr MELHUISH who Commands the Recon Coy. on April 26th & 27th Weather very fine during the month. Rain fell on 7 days only. | Appendix F. [signature] hujr L. O.C in I.F.A. |

Serial No. 154.

12/5/777

# WAR DIARY
## OF

112th Indian Field Ambulance. — Lahore Division

Lahore Division.

From 1st May. 1915 to 31st May. 1915.

May 1915

Army Form C. 2118.

# WAR DIARY
## or
## INTELLIGENCE SUMMARY.
*(Erase heading not required.)*

Pages 20—25

Instructions regarding War Diaries and Intelligence Summaries are contained in F. S. Regs., Part II. and the Staff Manual respectively. Title pages will be prepared in manuscript.

| Hour, Date, Place | Summary of Events and Information | Remarks and references to Appendices |
|---|---|---|
| | 112 INDIAN FIELD AMBULANCE LAHORE DIVISION I.E.F. May 1st — 31st 1915 | |

Army Form C. 2118.

# WAR DIARY
## or
## INTELLIGENCE SUMMARY.
(Erase heading not required.)

| Hour, Date, Place | Summary of Events and Information | Remarks and references to Appendices. |
|---|---|---|
| May 1st 1915. Boeschepe. | The unit marched from a Bivouack in a field 3/4 mile from Reninghelst on the Poperinghe road to a farm 3/4 mile to SE of BOESCHERE | Map BELGIUM Hazebrouck 5a. |
| May 2nd " | (Sunday) Sick for FEREZEPORE & JULLUNDUR Bde & 15 LANCERS. Received orders to hold in Readiness 1 No B BFA to Pt Mortier Via BERTHEN St Jans Cappel – BAILLEUL as to await orders there. The S.A. were transferred to our own Indn Ambulance to the clearing station. O/C MT DES CAT'S. The unit left BOESCHERE at 7:30 PM & was complealing delayed some after the start as the units in from had Rode in afth. only. Pt Mortier was Reached at 2.0 AM we soon after stabeled & off-seadied stuff the OC stated Duit Commanditc (Rum for the unit to Bread to CALONNE. The Colonne Reached by some two Bans at the unit auxiously Market CALONNE at 9.0 AM. The School Brooks Barn have been used by som of the French Cavaluries a small Barn was cut Rach and Re stabeled for a Refusal. Two Pres per.1 for Sub Ossiss Surgery O.S.C. Nin 5 of Appendix 5 for promulgation. Windy Sick for JULLUMDUR & FEREZEPORE Brigades. In opinion of YPRES & NERZB-30 | Appendix 5. Copy of letter O.C. 67 to ADMS LAHORE Div |
| May 3. CALONNE | | |
| May 4 " " | | |
| " 5 " | JULLUNDUR – FEREZEPORE - LA SIRHIND Brigades | |

# WAR DIARY
## or
## INTELLIGENCE SUMMARY.

*(Erase heading not required.)*

Army Form C. 2118.

Page 21.

| Hour, Date, Place | Summary of Events and Information | Remarks and references to Appendices |
|---|---|---|
| May 6th CALONNE 1915 | Orders from STRAND Bde. Regiment warned to march to billets in farms R 20 a 7.2. Marched at 10.0 p.m. in rear of No 6 B.F.A. via Petit Pacaut and L'EPINETTE. Arrived at post ordered by ADAMS (Telegs - 2nd & 6th) at 12.40 am & opened up quickly to form new lot. The lower company under Major McDOUGAL used by bodies to have all clear & write troops COLON M & S. In event | Map FRANCE (BETHUNE) 1/40,000 |
| " 7th CRON MA MUSE from R 20 a 72 | Called by side of SIRHIND Y FEROZE O.C. 3/3 am Rest. In [?] and part of JULL. Div. B. about [illegible] attacking pts | |
| " 7th | Called by side as above, at midnight Major McDOUGAL, Capt HELMA Assist Surg THANE—A Surg SUDARAM SAIN with 80 Recrs. of 4 N.M.R. arrived as draft at 5 pts M 27 d III when the lot Coms. were posted to the [illegible] the officers. Givers were STEWART & M.G. BHANDARI who should remain during the little explanation few were left in the trenches after the | |
| " 8th | During the night infantry attack but previously has fallen into the cool [illegible] fire company trenches & the advancing in-comment has been subjected to pts which were [illegible] Capt. [illegible] | |
| " 9th | During the day 72 wounded were placed at the first division | |
| " 10th | Dressing O.C. visits the advanced dressing Station [illegible] — Capt. NELSON — Asst Surg THANE & Sub Assn Surg SOULA [illegible] — Capt BOND — Lt STEWART & Sub Assn Surg [illegible]. Rem was followed by Capt ALI SAN. Under orders of the DDMS Indn Corps (Ad[?] 12 hrs) GOUHAL SINGH & ALI SAN were evacuated to STEWART in the future incapacity of the [illegible] | |

Army Form C. 2118.

Page 22.

# WAR DIARY
## or
## INTELLIGENCE SUMMARY.
*(Erase heading not required.)*

Instructions regarding War Diaries and Intelligence Summaries are contained in F.S. Regs., Part II. and the Staff Manual respectively. Title pages will be prepared in manuscript.

| Hour, Date, Place | Summary of Events and Information | Remarks and references to Appendices |
|---|---|---|
| May 11th Croix Barbasse | [illegible] Lt. ADAMS the local Camp [illegible] was withdrawn as the issue [illegible] Collection of Sick [illegible] was made from [illegible] and posts [illegible] hospital | |
| 12th " | Major ODLUM w Capt Sg Thyne visited the posts. | |
| 13th " | Major MELHUISH & Lt BHANDARI with S.A.S. SUDAMA RAM visited aid posts. | |
| 14th " | Major 13-14. Capt KELSALL visited aid posts. 14-15 " BOYD also Major ODLUM Bgd. [illegible] 15th Sikhs & BHANDARI Bgd. [illegible] 111 IFA | |
| 15th " | Major L.M. DEAS Appointed Div Surgeon. Major MELHUISH & Lt STEWART with Asst Sgs THYNE & SASSOON'S PAL with [illegible] [illegible] Company [illegible] left at 6.0 PM to form an advanced dressing station at Sy No 7 n.m. Beuvry Annex. | Map FRANCE (BETHUNE) 1/40,000 |
| 16th " | Lt. STEWART IMS [illegible] in departure to join the 40th Pathans (ADMS letter No 3/3 Aug 15) | |
| 17th " | [illegible] party [illegible] advanced dressing station [illegible] # 1 SAS 24 hrs will received outfit delivery (ADMS letter Div 282 15th Aug) | |
| 18th " | Captain BOND struck off duty in the field to join artillery of Divisional Cavalry. (A.D.M.S. letter Div. 47 16-8-15) | |
| 19th " | Major DEAS & Asst Sg THYNE visited aid posts at 9.30 pm. Return [illegible] | |
| 20th " | Major MELHUISH & SAS SURAJ PAL — ditto | |
| 21st " | Capt KELSALL & Asst Sg THYNE ditto | ditto |
| [illegible] " | A. EATON & SAS SUDAMA RAM ditto | ditto |
| [illegible] " | DEAS & SAS SUDAMA RAM ditto | ditto |

# WAR DIARY or INTELLIGENCE SUMMARY.

Army Form C. 2118.

Page 23.

| Hour, Date, Place | Summary of Events and Information | Remarks and references to Appendices |
|---|---|---|
| May 23rd CROIX MARMUSE 2.30 P.M. 1915 | Received orders to move out of Billets occupied as they were fitted for the Brigade Staff & area. Proceeded to pick up equipment etc. 7 wounded & 13 sick were evacuated by the convoy which Quickly arrived (as two of the wounded were serious). The remainder was taken along with unit, 12 wounded at 27 Suls. The Brigade indicated two small Barns on Sq R14 G.5.4. in which there was practically no accommodation under orders of A.D.M.S. the period here May June F 113 I.F.A. & this unit closed. Wounded were sent to be collected at the Point Ost Jakeh direct F 113. Arrived at new area at 5.30 P.M. | map FRANCE (Bethune) 1/40,000 |
| May 24. Sq R19.a. | Under orders of A.D.M.S. 8 sets were sent from 111 813 I.F.A. at a Camp Chat at left accommodt of Retained only. B Officer in dets G.o.S in a room in one of the barns, (men) Orders passed on these being 60 bers. A.S.C. men in Pass ambulances. Offices, gentm - sheet in R.o. Suitable Building Available. Major MELLWISH visited ard parts at 9.30 P.M. & Lub S/L & Lo. L of 113 I.F.A. |  |
| May 25. | O.C. of Capt. KELSALL visited the ard parts at dusk, a new portion of front having been taken up with fragmental and parts at S.3.572. It was deemed to evacuate the area of the tramway junction from the port as it was very open and the road from PONT LOGY to the port was found to be very open and a considerable number of rifle bullets were crossing it from the South & S.East it was also said to be often under shell fire. |  |

Army Form C. 2118.

Page 24.

# WAR DIARY
## or
## INTELLIGENCE SUMMARY.
*(Erase heading not required.)*

Instructions regarding War Diaries and Intelligence Summaries are contained in F. S. Regs., Part II. and the Staff Manual respectively. Title pages will be prepared in manuscript.

| Hour, Date, Place | Summary of Events and Information | Remarks and references to Appendices |
|---|---|---|
| May 26. Sq R 19 a. 1915 | Major MELHUISH inspected the Cable posts at 9.30 P.M. accompanied by Lieut. PATON | |
| " 27 " | The following is the present List of Officers in the Unit (F.A. order 552) | |
| | A Section - Captain R. KELSALL | |
| | Gov. SAS GAURI SHANKAR | |
| | 2 Class SAS SUDAMA RAM | |
| | P.S. Havildar LAL GUL (59 Rifles) | |
| | " " DEWA SINGH (57 Rifles) | |
| | Wd. Sirdar (54 Rifles) | |
| | " " NUR MOHD (54 Rifles) | |
| | B Section - Major H.M. MELHUISH | |
| | 3rd Class SAS SURAJ PAL | |
| | P.S. Havildar MOTA SINGH (15 Sikhs) | |
| | Wd. Sirdar RATTAN SINGH (6th Regt. ₺) | |
| | " " SADAR DIN (59 Rifles) | |
| | C Section - Major L.J.M. DEAS | |
| | (Capt. J.F. BOYD) | |
| | 1st Class SAS NARAYAN BAKSHAND SINGH | |
| | 3rd Class SAS ALI JAN | |
| | P.S. Havildar PUNJAB SINGH (59 Rifles) | |
| | Wd. Orderlie SHAH MOHD (37 Dogras) | |
| | " " SAJAWAL KHAN (52 Punjabis) | |
| | D Section - Lieut W.C. PATON | |
| | 2nd Class SAS AWANT PARAB | |
| | 3rd Class SAS GOKHAL SINGH | |
| | P.S. Havildar CHANNAN SINGH (47 Sikhs) | |
| | Wd. Sirdar PARTAB SINGH (34 Pioneers) | |
| | " " RAM ATAR (11th Rajputs) | |

**Army Form C. 2118.**

Pg 25.

# WAR DIARY
## or
## INTELLIGENCE SUMMARY.
*(Erase heading not required.)*

Instructions regarding War Diaries and Intelligence Summaries are contained in F.S. Regs., Part II. and the Staff Manual respectively. Title pages will be prepared in manuscript.

| Hour, Date, Place | Summary of Events and Information | Remarks and references to Appendices |
|---|---|---|
| 1915 | | |
| May 28th Sg R 19a | Appointments to Unit (Indian) | |
| " | Bearer Company. Majr H.M.MELHUISH  Lieut W.C. PATON | |
| " | Sub Asst Surg? GAURI SHANKAR — SURAJ PAL — ALI JAN — GORKHAL SINGH | |
| " | Ward Orderlies  DEWA SINGH — RATTAN SINGH — SHAH MOHD — PARTAB SINGH | |
| " | Cooks   ILLAHI DIN — MAHABIR, Bhistie MIRAM BAKHSH — PANNA | |
| " | Sweeper BHONDU — TULSI | |
| May 28th | Majr DEAS visits the aid posts which are open at dusk. Orders to rule | |
| 29th " | after HELSALL | ditto |
| 30th " | Indian orders 6 — the A.D.M.S. ( heavy 3B Dod) the unit loaded at 6.30 P.M. | |
|  | to LA GORGUE and open for reception of sick & wounded at the Boys School | |
|  | at 9.30 P.M. | |
|  | Genl PATON visited the aid posts which are open & dusk. | |
|  | Under special instructions from A.D.M.S. (324 Div) Majr DEAS proceeded to | |
| 31st LA GORGUE | the aid posts at 9.30 P.M. and collected sick & wounded awaiting for further | |
|  | reference the aid posts of the FEROZEPORE Bde who took over a | |
|  | certain portion & handed over the Run du Bois. | |
|  | Disp. the month 204 wounded & 322 Sick were passed through the Unit | |
|  | The weather was heavy & thundery at the beginning of the month but | |
|  | it was wet Mch 9 — 13th During the latter the weather was very bright | |
|  | & warm. | |

1-5-15.

To 2 I.F.A. Appendix 4

Under orders received from the A.D.M.S. LAHORE DIVISION, the Bearer Company marched from VLAMERTINGHE at 2-30 pm on 26-4-15 to open a Dressing Station at ST JEAN about a mile N.E. of YPRES. The usual equipment with the following personnel was taken —

MAJOR MELHUISH
LT. WALSH
SSN SAS GAURISHANKAR
S.A.S. ALI JAN
1 Pack & his Havildar
2 Ward Orderlies
85 Kahars with Stretchers.

Six Motor Ambulances were to have been taken over on the road from the F. Ambulance Camp to VLAMERTINGHE, but none of them having been removed & that some hit in dressing Station of No 3 F.A. they were unavailable. Half the equipment of the Bearer Company was put into these ambulances & the remainder returned to No 7 A.

ST JEAN we reached at 5 p.m. & a Dressing Station opened in 4 small houses on the SE side of the road from YPRES. Then walking each of the outposts & found many INDIAN wounded in that of the 40th PATHANS, & in the Dressing Station of No 10 F.A. I arranged immediately to remove as many as possible of the latter to my Dressing Station, while some of the 40th P. were sent off to the F.A. in the two motor ambulances. I then removed all wounded from the outposts of the 5th R Rifle, & the

for [?] only Defence Stores
[?] were [?] of the [?]
ED asking for as [?] a [?]
ambulances as [?] could be [?]
as for horse ambulances in
addition. After some time I obtained
4 [?] motor ambulances &
the 6 [?] available were
employed [?] for the next
few hours clearing my dressing
station which had been filled
with wounded & the [?] rather
first rate. I visited personally
[?] of the 89th RIFLES
9th BHOPAL INFANTRY, 15th SIKHS,
57th RIFLES, 1/1 GURKHAS &
1/9 GURKHAS. With the transport
at my disposal it was impossible
for me to evacuate any of the
wounded until early in the
morning of the 27th when I
put my motor ambulances at
the disposal of the MO 89th RIFLES

Have arrived here very exhausted. After daybreak on the 27th with the aid of D[?] form ambulances it was able tolerably clear all the wounded [?], except the BURKITTS who has very few wounded whom we do not do in any out but our dressing station remained full about all [to the] day. At 1 pm heavy shell fire [then] fell on the batteries in the immediate neighbourhood of the dressing station + at 2.30 pm the house itself was struck by 3 shells [?] killed and [?] slightly [?]. The personnel were mostly lying down under cover while the shelling continued & on the whole behaved with coolness. There were at this hour only a few sick in the dressing station, all wounded having been previously evacuated, but I decided to [move on to remove?] the dressing station to BRITSK[?]

a village about ¼ mile 15th W
[hole] was not best suitable &
could give no accommodation
[illegible] the place is being
filled with our own [illegible]. Had
Lt [illegible] Bruce Keland at this time
& CAPT KELSALL IMS, we
decided to refer the question to
the ADMS, and under his orders
the dressing station was withdrawn
to the Field Ambulance at
VLAMERTINGHE — one S.B. Post Sweeper
& two orderlies being left at
LA BRITRE.

The Staff worked well throughout
the period the dressing station was
open. I wish particularly to
notice Lt WALSH I.M.S.
   S.K.S ALI JAN
   Lee Naick GANESH RAM. A.B.C.

[signature]
Major
IMS

Appendix 5.  War Diary 112 I.F.A.  Jubbee Divn.

Copy of a Confidential letter OC 67 from the Officer Commanding 112 IFA to the ADMS LAHORE DIVN

Appendix 5

Reference your 28/28 of 2.5.1915

All ranks in this unit worked to their utmost and it is difficult to especially select names when all did well. Between 4.0 PM on April 26 and Noon on April 28th 863 wounded and 104 sick were admitted, and at one time between 350 and 450 wounded were in the unit. These large numbers were a severe test on the establishment both as regards (1) Surgical aid (2) Feeding and general care, supply of blankets and clean clothing etc where necessary (3) Records and clerical work.

Major H.M. McELHOSH as usual did exceptionally good work at the advanced dressing station which was frequently under shell fire, it was eventually hit and this Officer with commendable coolness transferred his personnel and certain sick which remained (the wounded having been evacuated) to the village of BRITKE. He acted all through with coolness and courage, April 26th & 27th. In his report he brings up the names of No 1335 3rd class SAS. SHEIKH ALI JAN for coolness & courage (appendix 4)  No 997 1st class SAS. NARAYAN PARSHAD SUROL as usual did most invaluable work at the Aid division, and to this man is due to a very large extent the smooth running of the interior economy of the unit, without which it would have been impossible to deal with such a large number of wounded in the short time without confusion. As it was each case was carefully shown on the A&D book, then passed on to one of the operating rooms where his wound was seen to and redressed if necessary, antitetanic serum given and clean clothing etc put on if considered advisable. From the operating rooms the cases passed to the wards where they received hot tea milk & food etc according to his condition. I strongly recommend NARAYAN PARSHAD for special notice.  No 321 2nd class SAS RAM KRISHNA ANANT PARAB who is in charge of the operating room showed conspicuous ability and merit during the period. All ranks worked continuously from midday on 26th to 8.0 PM on April 28th with only an allowance of 4 hours sleep during the period. Although no shells actually fell in the camp the adjacent village was frequently under shell fire during this time and a considerable number of shells fell in close proximity.

3.5.1915

Army Form C. 2118.

# WAR DIARY
## or
## INTELLIGENCE SUMMARY.
*(Erase heading not required.)*

Pages 26 — 31

112 Indian Field Ambulance

I.E.F.

June 1st to 30th 1915.

LAHORE DIVISION

June 1915

4 NOV 1919

From ADMS LAHORE DIVN "A" Form. Army Form C. 2121.
June 15.1915

## MESSAGES AND SIGNALS.

This message is on a/c of:
APPENDIX 6
original wire on 2 sheets

Secret.

TO: O.C. 112 I.F.A.

Sender's Number: 329
Day of Month: 15
AAA

Full Bearer Division No 112 IFA with two Officers & one half Bearer Division No 7 B.F.A. will rendezvous at 6.0 PM tonight at ST VAAST dressing station and collect wounded from area occupied by SIRHIND Bde AAA Full water cart from No 112 IFA to accompany Bearer Division AAA Motor ambulance waggons should not go forward till 6.30PM AAA 4 motor ambulance waggons of No 8 BFA are placed at disposal of O.C. No 112 IFA who will not send any more waggons forward than are necessary for evacuation of cases from dressing station AAA One half Bearer Division No 7 BFA under an officer will rendezvous at M 27 d dressing station at 6 PM & clear out posts on ESTAIRES LA BASSEE road AAA Full water cart of No 7 BFA to accompany this party AAA OC No 7 BFA will send two motor ambulance waggons to ST VAAST & two to M 27 d AAA British wounded to No 7 BFA Indian to No 112 IFA AAA The usual 6.0 AM noon & 4 PM wire rendered during operations will be sent to ADMS commencing 9.0 PM tonight AAA Reports to ADMS at ESTAIRES (on service) O.C. No 112 IFA will detail a Sub C[ffi]d Surgeon & one motor ambulance to take out British Wounded from M 27 d dressing station

From: ADMS
Place: ESTAIRES
Time: 8-15 PM

The above may be forwarded as now corrected. (Z)
Recd 6.0 PM.

Appendix 7 Correspondence on good work done under shell fire by men of No 112 I.F.A. on June 12, 1915

From M.O. 1st H.L.I.
To O.C. 112 I.F.A.

Sir - I have the honour to inform you of the excellent work done by the four stretcher bearers of your ambulance at our aid post on the 12th instance whilst the area around, and the road, was shelled. They gave us valuable assistance in attending to those wounded at the time and when conveying one B. Khan Khufa the shelling continued and as lead fell in 10 yards from them they calmly gave the patient the slightest inconvenience or did they waver till they carried him to a place of safety. Their conduct on this occasion was gratifying and I hope their work would permit them for their good service.

4349 Dvy Bearer MADHAM SINGH . 2354 Dvy Bearer CHHABO
3881 " RAKHIM KHAN 4397 " MASTNAN SINGH

Sd W WILKIE SCOTT
M.O. 1st H.L.I. & R.A.M.C

No 26/37 . 17.6.15
O.C. No 112 I.F.A.

Reference your No H31 d/ 17.6.15. These names will be noted for consideration when I am called upon by the Division to send in names for good work in the field. Have you might give each men 5 days from your friend at a parade of AB Corps men of your unit

Sd IAN SLOAN OCl
f/ Colonel Cdg ADMS Lahore Div

# WAR DIARY
## or
## INTELLIGENCE SUMMARY.
*(Erase heading not required.)*

Army Form C. 2118.

Page 26

| Hour, Date, Place | Summary of Events and Information | Remarks and references to Appendices |
|---|---|---|
| LA GORGUE. 1.6.1915 | The following arrangements for collection of Sick & Wounded from the units in the trenches were approved by the ADMS who will divide the posts with O.C.s No 7 & 112 F.As. 112 I.F.A. to collect both British and Indian from the aid posts along the Rue du Bois, Windy Corner (S 3 c 6.0) and Lansdowne (S 3 d 6.6) Area and bring them into the St VAAST post, on trestles when necessary. A Sub Assist Surgeon and orderly at 32 a.B.C. men with medical establishment of 1/2 bearer Coy. Equipment will be at the post. Sub A.B.C. men as are necessary will be left at each regimental aid post to bring wounded to the post as required. A British orderly will remain at the post to assist with British wounded. British orderlies will perform shell dressings and assist as Surgical dressings will be also an oxygen cylinder maintained at the post. The British and Indian Sick and Wounded from the LA BASSEE been fixed area will be collected by No 7 B.F.A. at held to their advanced dressing station of M 27 d. 112 I.F.A. is also called Sick from the aid posts at 9.30 P.M. Captain KELSALL availed the aid posts at 9.30 P.M. | Map FRANCE BETHUNE 1/40,000 |
| 2.6.1915 | Lieut PATON ditto | |
| 3.6.15 | Major DEAS ditto | |
| 4.6.15 | Major MELHUISH ditto | |
| 5.6.15 | Major KELSALL ditto especially visiting new aid posts as chancy of Bicycles to kick place. Captain R. KELSALL posted major of Brigades and Indian 360 of Oct 15.1915 | |

# WAR DIARY
## or
## INTELLIGENCE SUMMARY.
(Erase heading not required.)

Army Form C. 2118.

Page 27.

| Hour, Date, Place | Summary of Events and Information | Remarks and references to Appendices |
|---|---|---|
| LA GORGUE. 6.6.15 | Lieut PATON visited the aid posts under Lieut Allengreens | Map FRANCE BETHUNE (Second edition) 1/40,000 |
| 7.6.15 | Major DEAS ditto.  All aid posts in FRANCE (BETHUNE) (Sheet 1 edition) 6 pts its | |
| | Accepted maps changed by order of ADMS in the map (Sheet 1 edition) 6 pts its | |
| | use. 3 copies supplied to unit. | |
| 8.6.15 | O/C visited advd dress-station. Col Schultzf. Major KELSALL visited aid posts | |
| 9.6.15 | Asst Sug W.K. WISEMAN effected li-aumd. Asst Sug W.H. THYNE left for No 20 B.F.A. | |
| | Lieut PATON visited the aid posts under advd dressgts. | |
| 10.6.15 | Major H.M. MELHUISH effected his departure to take over command of No III L.F.A. | |
| | With ADMS, LAHORE Dept order No 37. | |
| | Major DEAS visited the aid posts under advd arrangements. Qublin of note. | |
| 11.6.15 | Major KELSALL ditto | |
| 12.6.15 | Lieut PATON ditto | |
| 13.6.15 | Major DEAS ditto | |
| 14.6.15 | Major KELSALL ditto | |
| 15.6.15 | under orders from the ADMS the full bearer Coy pay under Major KELSALL took Lieut PATON of Sub Assistant Surgeon ALI JAN of SUDAMA RAM proceeded to the advanced dressing section at ST VAAST leaving this old O.D P.M. | ADMS Gds Div hunng 329. Appendix B. attached. |
| | Captain CH. REINHOLD was joined for temp duty. | |
| | Up to the commencement of this operation the unit has had in 101 | |
| | Wd Cases and 165 Cases of Sickness during the month. | |
| | After commence of [illegible] on the date 8 wounded were admitted | |

Army Form C. 2118.

Page 28.

# WAR DIARY
## or
## INTELLIGENCE SUMMARY.
(Erase heading not required.)

Instructions regarding War Diaries and Intelligence Summaries are contained in F.S. Regs., Part II. and the Staff Manual respectively. Title pages will be prepared in manuscript.

| Hour, Date, Place | Summary of Events and Information | Remarks and references to Appendices |
|---|---|---|
| LA GORGUE. 16.6.15 | Major KELSALL reports all quiet during the night and no extra enemy aeroplanes at the dressing station and posts. Indus orders by A.D.M.S. (Major 340) the becan (empty) was withdrawn and the issue arrangements as ruled under date 1.6.15 were resumed from 7.0 P.M. 6 wounded admitted during the day. | |
| 17.6.15 | Captain REINHOLD visited the out posts at 9.30 P.M. not - 2 not. ditto | |
| 18.6.15 | Captain PATON ditto | |
|  | Major DEAS reported for attachment for 7 days leave. With the approval of the ADMS a parade was held at noon and the bretheren were presented with 5 francs each from the Indian Relief Fund for conduct reflecting credit on the Army Bearer Corps on June 12, when they gave first assistance to the M.O. 1st Highland L.I. in France, wounded from the regimental aid post to place of safety under heavy shell fire. Copy HLI letter attached. Their names have been noted by A.D.M.S. M.O. | 2 appendices |
|  | No 4349 Bearer MADHAN SINGH No 2 Co No. 4597 MASTAN SINGH No 4 Co | |
|  | No 2354 " CHABU No 2 Co No 3861 RAKHINA KHAN No 3 Co | |
| 19.6.15 | Major KELSALL visited the out posts at 9.30 P.M. not - 2 not. (Major) Sub Asst Surg. NARAYAN PARSHAD SUKUL assumed the duties of Distn guard Serai behind Alins. the first distribution guard by the Hindu since the commencement of the war i.e. Sub Asst Surg. CHURA HAMAR and No 4309 Naik MADANA (invalided) the Serai is temporarily being looked in two. | |

**Army Form C. 2118.**

Page 29.

# WAR DIARY
## or
## INTELLIGENCE SUMMARY.
*(Erase heading not required.)*

Instructions regarding War Diaries and Intelligence Summaries are contained in F.S. Regs., Part II. and the Staff Manual respectively. Title pages will be prepared in manuscript.

| Hour, Date, Place | Summary of Events and Information | Remarks and references to Appendices |
|---|---|---|
| LA GORGUE 20.6.15 | O.C. with Major KELSALL visited aid posts along the whole of stationed by JULLONDUR Bde at midnight. | |
| 21.6.15 | Captain REINHOLD visited the aid posts at 9.30 P.M. none of note. | |
| 22.6.15 | Lieut PATON ditto | |
| 23.6.15 | Major KELSALL ditto nothing especially the heavy Division tends to a stroke over some of the front | |
| 24.6.15 | Under orders of A.D.M.S. the S.Vraast dressing station was converted at 5.30 P.M. and a combined dress. station formed at M 27.d with No 7 B.F.A. Captain Reinhold visited the dress. station at 10.0 P.M. and got into touch with the units of the Division which remained in the S.VAAST area. No 7 B.F.A. returned to clear the LA BASSEE dist. aid posts. Major DEAS after his return from 7 days leave. Captain REINHOLD rejoined III I.F.A. under orders from A.D.M.S. Capt PATON visited the aid posts and got into touch with the units of the JULLUNDUR Bde. FEROZEPORE Bde on MANCHESTER Regt. The remainder of the JULLUNDUR Bde. relieved as before by No 7 B.F.A. | Map FRANCE. BETHUNE (Servir edition) 40,000 |
| 26.6.15 | Major DEAS visited the aid posts between 10.0 P.M. at 1.0 A.M. Jullundur Bde. Sir James Willcocks visited the wounded during the forenoon. | |
| 27.6.15 | O.C. visited the regimental aid posts in the Rue de Bacquerot area with the A.D.M.S. Stella Divn during the morning. All quiet at the time Major KELSALL visited the aid posts at 10.0 P.M. midnight rds. A.D. | |

# WAR DIARY or INTELLIGENCE SUMMARY

Army Form C. 2118.
Page 30

| Hour, Date, Place | Summary of Events and Information | Remarks and references to Appendices |
|---|---|---|
| 26.6.1915 LA GORGUE | Issued orders to the G.O.C. Divn (ADMS [indistinct] 44/33 of date) hand wounds are to be retained in F.A. with the exception of serious hand wounds, for example — 9.0 AM 27th to 9.0 AM 28th out of 33 Gunshot wounds 17 were wounds of hand & forearm. Lt PATON visited the SIRHIND B.H. and posts under which enquiries. Bathey Jb orde. (FEROZEPORE Relieved by SIRHIND ADMS missing 360 "B" class) | |
| 29.6.15. | out of 46 wound cases admitted since 9.0 AM on 28th 17 are wounds of hand at 9 of forearm. Lieut J.C. JOHN IMS reported for arrived for temprary duty. Major DOGRA at Lt JOHN visited the civil posts under reserve arrangements, incl. Sp posts. | |
| 30.6.15. | 25 wound cases out of which 5 Hav & 9 Forearm. Major HELSALL visited the civil posts under which attempts at 10.0 PM. The No 50 wounded admitted during the week was 384 " Sick 363 Ditto Sick. The following were the posting in the last during the month [A] Section: Major R. KELSALL, S.A.S. GAURI SHANKAR, Hav. LAL GUL (59th R.) [W.O. indistinct] DEWA SINGH 57th Rifles FF [B] Section: Major G. BROWSE S.A.S.(?) SUDAMA RAM - 1406 SURAI PAL Hav. MOTA SINGH (15.S) W.O. RATTAN SINGH (8 R) NUR MAHO (59 R) [C] Major L.J.M. DEAS (Surgyn) Captain J.F. BOYD (Dr. duty with Divnl Batts) 1335 S.A.S. NARAYAN PARSHAD SUKUL - ALI JAN . Hav PUNJAB SINGH (59 R) | |

Army Form C. 2118.

Page 31.

# WAR DIARY
## or
## INTELLIGENCE SUMMARY.
*(Erase heading not required.)*

| Hour, Date, Place | Summary of Events and Information | Remarks and references to Appendices |
|---|---|---|

Postings during June contd.

[D] Section. Lt W.C. Paton   S.A.S. Anant Parab 133b — Gokhal Singh 321

No. Channan Singh (42S)   W.O. Partab Singh (34P.) Ram Atar (11R)

[Bearer Co.]   Major R. Kelsall   S.A.S. Gauri Shankar
Lt W.C. Paton                Ali Jani
                             Gokhal Singh
                             Suraj Pal

W.Os Dewa Singh — Rattan Singh
    Shah Mohd — Partab Singh

Cooks. Mam Din — Mahabir   Bhestis Kiran Bakhsh  Sweepers Bhondu
                                     Tamma                   Tulsi

Weather. 1st fortnight Fine & Hot.   10–11 Heavy thunder shower, dust & rain.
12–21 Fine — Hot.   21–30. Showery & colder.

A large number of mosquitos all the month, mostly Culex. C. fr. A Maculipennis were caught only in the month, & were seen after the middle of the month.

C.B. Beats
Major w.
O.C. 1/2 V.F.A.

Serial No. 154.

121/6502

July 15

# WAR DIARY

## 112 Indian Field Ambulance.

FROM 1st July 1915 TO 31st July 1915

Army Form C. 2118.

P 32

# WAR DIARY
## or
## INTELLIGENCE SUMMARY.
(Erase heading not required.)

Instructions regarding War Diaries and Intelligence Summaries are contained in F.S. Regs., Part II. and the Staff Manual respectively. Title pages will be prepared in manuscript.

| Hour, Date, Place | Summary of Events and Information | Remarks and references to Appendices |
|---|---|---|
| July 1st 1915 LA GORGUE | Lieut JOHN visited A&E and posts at 9.30 P.M. under usual arrangements. Route of return 9.0 A.M. on 30th to 9.0 A.M. 1st no.1 of 9 wounded cases admitted 2 knee wound below elbow. | |
| 2nd " | Lieut CATON Spoke on disposition on 7 days leave. Major DEAS visited A&E and posts at 9.30 P.M. under usual arrangements. Route of return. out of 29 wounded admitted in the 24 hrs — 12 knee below forearm until advanced dressing station while Off Cdr SLOAN. Slight burst until dressing shed fin. | |
| 3rd " 4.30 P.M. | Major KELSALL visited A&E and posts under usual arrangements Route of return out of 16 wounded admitted 6 knee below forearm. | |
| 4th " | Major KELSALL visited A&E and posts at 9.30 P.M. accompanied by OC to verify the positions of all the light section and posts on the BETHUNE 40.50 Map. Route of return. Loaned 5. only 1 below forearm. | |
| 5th " | Lieut JOHN visited A&E and posts under usual arrangements. Route of return. Wounded 11. None below forearm. | |
| 6th " | Major DEAS visited A&E and posts under usual arrangements. Route of return wounds 9. 2 below forearm. | |
| 7th " | Lt JOHN visited A&E and posts under usual arrangements. Route of return wounds 11. 1 below forearm. | |
| 7th " | Major KELSALL Commanding held a meeting at 9 A.M. by order of ADMS Below forearm. Route of return. | |
| 8th — | Major DEAS visited A&E and posts under usual arrangements. Route of return. Below forearm wd. at M25 d.7.3 | |

Major KELSALL

Army Form C. 2118.

P 33.

# WAR DIARY
## or
## INTELLIGENCE SUMMARY.
(Erase heading not required.)

Instructions regarding War Diaries and Intelligence Summaries are contained in F.S. Regs., Part II and the Staff Manual respectively. Title pages will be prepared in manuscript.

| Hour, Date, Place | Summary of Events and Information | Remarks and references to Appendices |
|---|---|---|
| July 9. LA GORGUE 19.15 | Lt JOHN visited the aid post. Later the transport sheds at 9.30 P.M. Maj. S. 4 was Maj. KELSALL with the dug out on M 28 d. 7.3 | Map FRANCE ("B" Series) BETHUNE 1/40,000 |
| 10 | O.C. visited M 28 d 7.3 at 10.30 A.M. Heavy Prussian shell [fell?] Irregularly about 100 yds in front at 200 to 250 yds in rear of the position. The farm on plain side of AUBERS ridge but the dug outs are being well sheltered by a slight mound. Some Gales, R.H.A, B AUBERS Church 85° true N. Maj. KELSALL assisted Mr Van Helleburg for [?] about an hour, till dug R.A.S.F. hands himself to A.D.M.S. Maj. DEAS visited the aid post at 4.30 P.M. moved if made. |  |
|  | Level 7. Held N [?] Coml 1. |  |
| 11 | Maj. DEAS visited the aid post at 9.30 noon passing by Lt Colonel A.J MACNAB and [?] note. | 1836 |
|  | Maj. KELSALL inspected the dug out on M 28 M 28 d 7.3 they were lightly gassing. There was heavy Prussian fire round the position during the day. Report to A.D.M.S. |  |
| 12 | Lt PATON visited the aid post at 10.15 P.M. [?] [?] [?] Level 8. Held Journal 2. |  |
| 13 | Maj KELSALL and [?] [?] Level 5. Held B [?] 1. | C.M.S. |

(73989) W4141-463. 400,000. 9/14. H.&J.Ltd. Forms/C. 2118/10.

Army Form C. 2118.

Page 34

# WAR DIARY
## or
## INTELLIGENCE SUMMARY.
(Erase heading not required.)

Instructions regarding War Diaries and Intelligence Summaries are contained in F. S. Regs., Part II. and the Staff Manual respectively. Title pages will be prepared in manuscript.

| Hour, Date, Place | Summary of Events and Information | Remarks and references to Appendices |
|---|---|---|
| 14.7.15 LA GORGUE | O.C. with Major KELSALL accompanied A.D.M.S. to ammunition station at 11.0 a.m. and met R.E. Officer there. Arrangements made clearing huts in gun end on S.W. side of Buildings work set on. Practicable openings in walls. Major KELSALL to supervise alterations with O.C. F.A. & saw O/C A.S.C. & Lieut POPE J. F.A. Jnr of R.E. at 11 a.m. 73 O/J PATCH visited the road past to 4.30 p.m. Road very muddy. | |
| 15.7.15 " | The O/c Orus, Sec. filled mostly Spare tops prepared equipment and installed prepared on return to [?] N.G.G.F.A. at 4.30 p.m. No's Left Dm [?] 20 [?] shock firing. Completion of the day out. [?] Change of SF to G Lieut. Walsh known with the 35th [?] 34 [?] is [?] Sub Field Ambulance H.F.A. Albion etc. | |
| 16.7.15 " | Major KELSALL ret. at 11 p.m. A.S.C. [?] the field by Saturday No 4951. Sepoy had duties MUKAT SINGH 16 Rajputs reported arrived for duty. The two sepoys Khoyla Ali who had no medical training had seemed that, One of the Second Lieutenants was Aleg [?] received from the Base (22nd) Sepoy RAMDYAS SINGH 11 Raj [F.G. dated 10.7.15] on 15.2.15) a report sent to A.D.M.S. Afghan Div. (S.G.61 dated 10.7.15) pointing out that in addition to A.S.G. dust without Rifles or Bayonets, he was bound to all posts must be escorted out of the man to be allowed to the Field Ambulance train Afghan attached to the Section [?] under the Surgeon Specialist for Special Training. | A.D.M.S. Lahore Div No. 34/167. 16.7.15 [signature] |

(73989) W4141—463. 400,000. 9/14. H.&J.Ltd. Forms/C. 2118/10.

Army Form C. 2118.

Pay 35.

# WAR DIARY
## or
## INTELLIGENCE SUMMARY.
(Erase heading not required.)

Instructions regarding War Diaries and Intelligence Summaries are contained in F.S. Regs., Part II and the Staff Manual respectively. Title pages will be prepared in manuscript.

| Hour, Date, Place | Summary of Events and Information | Remarks and references to Appendices |
|---|---|---|
| LA GORGUE 17.7.15 | Collecting Sick & wounded as on 16th inst - 10 mitt. | |
| " 18.7.15 | ditto | |
| " 19.7.15 | ditto | |
| | Completed the work at M27 & M28d. There was also some further work to be done at M28d in Suffolk Ave opposite the junction of the farm track KELSALL road apart from led Culbent thro' open with heavy shell fire. On completion the men came to N track ove of in times. Bringing up the gear two huge KELSALL road as narrow escape a high explosive shell bursting close to him. Considerable dampness & casualties to some horses. | |
| 20.7.15 | Collecting sick & wounded as above. had - 7 mitt. | ADMS 20/7/15 |
| " 21.7.15 | ditto | |
| | Had orders to ADMS with M.O.C. S/3 & one horse KELSALL to carry for cleanings up at what has been received. Divnl Staff for Brigade Dublin Suk & wounded from the N Section of the line to be held by the Division. A Sub asst Surgn (SUBAS DAS) with Sweepers & other personnel sent up to CROIX BARBEE. | 20.7.15 |
| 22.7.15 | Collecting Sick as above. Work at M.O.C. Continued under Capt KELSALL | eul. |

# WAR DIARY or INTELLIGENCE SUMMARY

Army Form C. 2118.

P 3/5

| Hour, Date, Place | Summary of Events and Information | Remarks and references to Appendices |
|---|---|---|
| LA GORGUE 22.7.15 | Maj. DEAS & Lt. PATON proceed at 9.30 p.m. to recce the lignes of the SIRHIND Bde who have taken over the COLVIN TRENCH (exclusive) to FAUQUISSART AUBERS Road. Also taken over the Northern Section & British & Indian kits in this section. The Southern Section, LA BASSEE road to COLVIN TRENCH (both inclusive) is being cleared by No 6 B.F.A. & the GREEN BARN advanced dressing station is left as 73 JULLUNDUR Bde H.q. Cattle Section. O/c and Lecure Section with Assist Surgn - Sub Assist Surgn & personnel return at end of dressing station. M.I.O. & M.2 & 10 as the Med wale both British & Indian Sick & wounded. Head over 8 & 9 Sick admitted during the 24 hrs. Collect sick as above. Maj KELSALL visited N Section mid points at 9.30pm | ADMS LAHORE ON leaving 360 dated 22.7.15 JULLUNDUR. 1 Manchesters 4 Suffolks 1 Seaforth 4 Seaforths 47 Sikhs 59 Rifles 2/8 Gurkhas 64 Rifles 39 Gurkhas SIRHIND 1 H.L.I. 4 Kings 2 Leicester 57 Rifles 3 London |
| 23.7.15 | 7 wounded & 11 sick admitted during the 24 hrs. | |
| 24.7.15 | Out-puts as above. Lt PATON visited mid & points. Maj. G. BROWSE M.I.Z.I. returns on 7 days leave. 2 wounded, 15 sick during the 24 hrs. | |
| 25.7.15 | Out-puts as above. Maj DEAS visited mid and points. 6 wounded 5 sick during 24 hrs. | |
| 26.7.15 | Out-puts as above. Maj KELSALL visited mid and points. 19 wounded 12 sick ditto | |
| 27.7.15 | Out-puts as above. Maj PATON visited mid and points. 8 sick ditto | |
| 28.7.15 | Out-puts as above. Maj DEAS visited mid and points. 5 sick ditto. 10 sick ditto | |
| 29.7.15 | Out-puts as above. Maj KELSALL visited mid and points. 19 wounded 14 sick ditto | |

Army Form C. 2118.

Pay 37.

# WAR DIARY
## or
## INTELLIGENCE SUMMARY.
(Erase heading not required.)

| Hour, Date, Place | Summary of Events and Information | Remarks and references to Appendices |
|---|---|---|
| LA GORGUE 30.7.1915 | The foregoing collection of Sick & wounded returned in addition to which the BAREILLY Bde sent in the area of Some of this trench will go into the trenches in relief of SIRHIND with a the latter will now Back into billets so will have to be paid for Sick. Major SEAS MAZZI and parts of 9.30 P.M. LUFS SICS along the ref. | ADMS Lahore Div Mhow(?) 386 / 30/7/15 BAREILLY 2 Bareilland 1/4 others 41 Dogras 58 Rifles 59 Punjabis |
| 31.7.1915 | Proceeded to about the FERROZEPORE & GARHWAL Brigades now into area. Ferozepore 1 Batt Sirhid relieve Jullunder at the latter go into billets so will be billets for Sick. The Garhwal Brigade relieve Bareilly in area COLVIN that to WINCHESTER Road so that 5 latter will leave the trench for Sick. In the 7 Sics 23 along the res. This Bde is now relieving Sick & wounded from the stand area FAUQUISSART to COLVIN TRENCH and the Sick of 9 Indian Div is B 5 Brigade, will post both Divls Drs & Amps & 2 Divisions. During the month 282 Sick & 217 wounded men proceeded to the unit. Weather up to 15th fine 16-17 cold & showery then it could mostly fine with occasional showers. | ADMS Lahore Div Listings 391 $ 31/7/15 GARHWAL 2 Leicesters 3 Gurkhas 2/3 GR 49 GR FEROZEPORE Connaughts 4 Suffolks 57 Rifles 129 Baluch 40 Pathans |

C.J.Sanderson Lt Col
ADMS LFA

Aug '15.

Serial No 154.

124/6948
127/6958

# WAR DIARY
## OF

112 Indian Field Ambulance, Lahore Division.

FROM 1st August 1915 TO 31st August 1915

Army Form C. 2118.

Page 36.

# WAR DIARY
## or
## INTELLIGENCE SUMMARY.
(Erase heading not required.)

| Hour, Date, Place 1915. | Summary of Events and Information | Remarks and references to Appendices |
|---|---|---|
| LA GORGUE August 1. | Collection of Sick & wounded as under July 31. Major KELSALL took over the advanced dress. Station at St VAAST at 10.0 AM. The wound staffs and equipment placed there. (1 SAS. 1 WO 20 ABC & Menial establisht.) Major KELSALL visited the aid posts closed to about post at 9.30 PM. One post at LANSDOWNE S.3.d.6.6 & two at the Bran Road about S.10.a.5.3. Major DEAS visited the aid posts closed to the LA FLINQUE dress. Station MID.C.5.1 at 9.30 PM. Sick 29 wounded 12 during the 24 hours. | ADMS Lahore Div. letter 396. 31.7.15  ADMS Lahore Div. letter 397. 1.8.15 |
| " Aug 2. | The post at LA FLINQUE handed over to the MEERUT DIV at 10.0 AM by Major KELSALL. Sick 4 wounded 9 during the 24 hours. Major PATON visited the aid posts closed by the S.VAAST Station. | ADMS Lahore Div. letter 401. 1.8.15 |
| " Aug 3. | Major DEAS visited above aid posts at 9.0 PM. Sick 7 wounded 5 during the 24 hours. | |
| " Aug 4. | Visited S.VAAST post wall off (Col SLOAN) & Major DEAS to arrange abt dugout splinter proof shelters. 5.0 PM. Major PATON visited the aid posts as above at 9.30 PM. Sick 3 wounded 12 during the 24 hours. Major KELSALL After lis departure for on weeks leave. | |
| " Aug 5. | Major BROWSE visited the aid posts as above accompanied by an Officer from a 19th Div F.A for instructional purposes. Major DEAS & a fatigue party incl. shelters at S.VAAST. Sick 3 wounded 3 during the 24 hours. | |
| " Aug 6 | Major PATON visited the aid posts as above by an officer fr the 19th Div F.A. Sick 14 wounded 6 during the 24 hours. Major DEAS continues work & made & sketch & splinter proof shelters at S.VAAST. | |

Army Form C. 2118.

P.39

# WAR DIARY
## or
## INTELLIGENCE SUMMARY.
(Erase heading not required.)

Instructions regarding War Diaries and Intelligence Summaries are contained in F.S. Regs., Part II. and the Staff Manual respectively. Title pages will be prepared in manuscript.

| Hour, Date, Place | Summary of Events and Information | Remarks and references to Appendices |
|---|---|---|
| LA GORGUE 7.8.1915 | Major DEAS continuing the digging of splinter proof shelters at S.VAAST. Major BROWSE the improved aid posts accepted by a Major from a F.A. 6 the 19th Div for instructional purposes. 9.30 PM Sgt JAMES WILCOCKS unspiked the cartridges at 3.30 PM. Sick 8 wounded 11 during the 24 hours. | Manchester Regt. Lansdowne Post 59 & 47 Combined S.9 d 119 |
| 8.8.1915 | Digging of shelters at S.VAAST continued. Major BROWSE visited the aid posts at 9.30 PM on closing the position of the JULLUNDUR BDE who were following the SIRHIND Bde. Sick 5 wounded 3 accidents during the 24 hours. |  |
| 9.8.15 | Shelters at S.VAAST completed in turn Jacky Sgt Yardley of F.C. R.E. Lt PATON visited the aid posts at 9.30 PM. Sick 5 wounded 6 accidents during the 24 hours. |  |
| 10.8.15 | Major DEAS visited the aid posts at 9.30 PM hallis wood letter grounds. Sick 13 wounded 5 unfit td club of the 24 hours. |  |
| 11.8.15 | Major BROWSE visited the aid posts at 9.30 PM when order not spiked Sick 7 wounded 6 admitted during the 24 hours. Major KELSALL departed on course for 7 days' leave. |  |
| 12.8.15 | Lt PATON visited the aid posts at 9.30 PM wounded issued Enlargements Sick 2 wounded 2 accidents during the 24 hours. |  |
| 13.8.15 | Indian Indian from the A.D.M.S. (dated 4.8.15) (vide) Major KELSALL handed over the advanced dressing station at S.VAAST at noon to III F.A. This unit closed from Aire Anne. A party of 20 A.S.C. men under G March serving at S.VAAST to continue work in the Bomb proof Shelters under Major KELSALL. |  |

Army Form C. 2118.

# WAR DIARY
## or
## INTELLIGENCE SUMMARY.
*(Erase heading not required.)*

Page 40.

Instructions regarding War Diaries and Intelligence Summaries are contained in F.S. Regs., Part II. and the Staff Manual respectively. Title pages will be prepared in manuscript.

| Hour, Date, Place | | Summary of Events and Information | Remarks and references to Appendices |
|---|---|---|---|
| LA GORGUE. | 14.8.15 | Units closed. Out in B. route. Party at S.VAAST incl't Bond (D.M) Shelters. | |
| " | 15.8.15 | Ditto. Ditto - (O.C. inspected shelters with Major KELSALL) | |
| " | 16.8.15 | Lt PATON joined the 59 Rfls F.F. for training duty (ADM's Message 39/98 15.6.15) Routine drill & instruction commenced. | |
| | | Coy'y & Sketcher drill 9-10 AM. 1st Cav'd to W.O.Schedule, ABC NCOs at the numbers from 10 c.d. Stretcher Sqns. 11.10 AM to Noon Under Sup Spencely. Instruction to B.Os S.A.S. without Stretcher and check by equipment & duties. Under section arrangements. | |
| | 17.8.15 | Ditto as above route - B. route | |
| | 18.8.15 | Ditto " | |
| | 19.8.15 | Ditto " | |
| | 20.8.15 | Ditto " | |
| | 21.8.15 | Ditto " | |
| | 22.8.15 | O.C. accompanied by Major KELSALL inspected the shelters, when placed along the LA BASSEE road about 12.45 pm at M 27 d 6.7 (approximate) a large high explosive shell fell at the corner of the Lorette Rd a frag'ty which struck Major KELSALL on the shoulder inflicting a severe bruise only. | Map FRANCE (Bethune) 1/3 Scale 10.000 |
| | 23.8.15 | Routine drill & instruction as above. Parties at Open Barn & S.VAAST under Major KELSALL continuing the making of Bond (D.M) shelters as above. | |
| | 24.8.15 | Ditto | |
| | 25.9.15 | Ditto | |

(73989) W4141—463. 400,000. 9/14. H.&J.Ltd. Forms/C. 2118/10.

Army Form C. 2118.

# WAR DIARY
## or
## INTELLIGENCE SUMMARY.
(Erase heading not required.)

Page 41.

| Hour, Date, Place | | Summary of Events and Information | Remarks and references to Appendices |
|---|---|---|---|
| LA GORGUE | 26.8.1915 | Under instruction fr ADMS Major L.J.M. DEAS prepared his departure to take over command of 129 I.F.A. (ADMS Lahore Dn message 31/37. 25-8-15) | |
| " | 27.8.1915 | Routine work as above | |
| " | 27.8.2 | ditto | |
| | | Under orders of ADMS (message 447, 27.8.15) the unit marched to | |
| CALONNE | 28.8. | CALONNE and opened (by the Baptism of Hand & Jeroboam Cases under enemy in the side of the SIRHIND Bde in the school @ 3 d 6.3 | Map FRANCE (B series) Sheet 36A 1/40,000 |
| " | 29.8. | Ditto march 1 mile | |
| " | 30.8.? | Ditto Ditto | |
| " | 31.8.? | Weather during the month. Hot & Sultry with some cloud fr Aug 1 to 13th then to 17th Showers. Drizzle & colder 18th to 21st 22 to 28th fine & sunny generally. 29 to 31 wet & cold. | |

C. B. Younghusband
O.C. 111 I.F.A.

121/7286

Serial No. 154

# WAR DIARY

## OF

112th Indian Field Ambulance.

FROM 1st September 1915 TO 30th September 1915

Army Form C. 2118.

Pg 42

# WAR DIARY
## or
## INTELLIGENCE SUMMARY.
(Erase heading not required.)

Instructions regarding War Diaries and Intelligence Summaries are contained in F.S. Regs., Part II. and the Staff Manual respectively. Title pages will be prepared in manuscript.

| Hour, Date, Place | Summary of Events and Information | Remarks and references to Appendices |
|---|---|---|
| Sept 1. 1915. CALONNE | Q3 cl. 6.3. Units open for Cand & General Cases as before. Note Yvorte. Also Sens. Dairy Sick of 4th Dvn Supply Column w/ dispersing cases for admission to No 58 F.A. | Map FRANCE (13 Sens) Sheet 36 A. 1/40,000 |
| " 2 | | |
| " 3 | Ditto. Part II orders. MT 11566 Pte DORVILLE .G. rejoining from Conv Co | |
| | MERVILLE | |
| " 4 | Ditto | |
| " 5 | Ditto. Part II orders. Gunr W.C. PATON has Having been transferred. Sick to Struck off the strength of the unit. | |
| " 6 | Ditto | |
| " 7 | Ditto | |
| " 8 | Ditto. Part II Sick as. M.T 03306 Pte J.A. SHAW transferred Sick to No 6 B.F.A. Struck off strength 1 wait from 7.9.1915. | |
| " 9 -" 12 | Ditto. Little of note | |
| " 13. | On addition to above the Sick of Works/Baths– Collected cooking in admitted | |
| " 14 | Ditto. Part II orders. No. 4 Cook Pre Ashton transferred to hospital. Convoy Clerk, Sgt ...... | |

(73989) W4141–463. 400,000. 9/14. H.&J.Ltd. Forms/C. 2118/10.

# WAR DIARY
## or
## INTELLIGENCE SUMMARY.
*(Erase heading not required.)*

Army Form C. 2118.

Pg 43.

| Hour, Date, Place | Summary of Events and Information | Remarks and references to Appendices |
|---|---|---|
| Sept 15 CALONNE 1915 | Taking hand wounds from III I.F.A. as before. All the sick & walking Battal. also sick daily sick of 19th Divn Supply Column. | |
| " 16 " | Ditto. Part II orders. Sergt. J. BAKER reported arrival from No 7 B.F.A. in place of Sergt F. REILLY M.T. A.S.C. | |
| " 17 " | Ditto. | |
| " 18 " | Ditto. Part II orders. MT/07885 Sergt J. BAKER A.S.C. w Sergt A. WATKINS (E near Regt) SVT Sergt in the List transferred sick to No 8 B.F.A. No 3046 Havildar KISHEN CHAND 27th Punjabis reported sick. | |
| " 19 " | Ditto. Part II orders. No 4036 Naick SHAMA is promoted to acting Lce Havildar from 8/9/10 vice Lce Hav Havildar MANSOOH transferred sick on march 10— No 1721 P.S. Havildar BIR SINGH GURUNG rejoined the 1/1 G. Rifles. | |
| " 20 " | Ditto. Part II orders. Captn A. KENNEDY I.M.S. reported for duty. | CMS |
| " 21 " | Ditto with 1 rank. | |
| " 22 " | Ditto. Ditto. | |

# WAR DIARY or INTELLIGENCE SUMMARY

Army Form C. 2118.
Page 44.

| Hour, Date, Place | Summary of Events and Information | Remarks and references to Appendices |
|---|---|---|
| Sept 23. CROIX MARMUSE 1915 | Under orders of ADMS (message 474/22.9.15) The Unit marched to CROIX MSE to form R.I.O.C 6.8 & opened to receive the sick of the Division 10.30 AM to noon. 2 sick called & evacuated. | |
| " 24 " | Under Confidential orders of ADMS (Operation orders 48 dated 23.9.15) Captains BOYD & KENNEDY – Sub Assist Surgeons GAURI SHANKAR – ALI JAN GORHAL SINGH & SURAJ PAL – And Orderlies SADU SINGH – MOHAT SINGH YUSAF KHAN with 90 bearers & 20 stretchers upstart to bvegue O.C. 111 I.F.A at 2.30 PM 4 Motor ambulances reported to O.C. 111 I.F.A at 9.0 AM & one Lux ambce to O.C. No 8 B.F.A. Captains J.F.BOYD IMS & Captain H.WATTS IMSrelue After arrival for duty. 27 Cases of Sickness admitted | |
| " 25 " | Under 1 mote 12 Cases of Sickness admitted | |
| " 26 " | Under 1 mote 12 cases ditto | |
| " 27 " | Captains BOYD & KENNEDY 11 Cases of Sickness admitted returned to the unit as Captain WATTS rejoined the Division H.Q. | |
| " 30 " | The remainder of the personnel & Ambulance back to 111 I.F.A returned Lcal or duty BURA SINGH (3rd duty) joined for duty 16 cases of Sickness admitted | |

O.S.

Army Form C. 2118.

# WAR DIARY
## or
## INTELLIGENCE SUMMARY.
*(Erase heading not required.)*

Page 45.

| Hour, Date, Place | Summary of Events and Information | Remarks and references to Appendices |
|---|---|---|
| Sept 29. CROIX MARMUSE 1915 | The unit closed for inspection of Sick during the week by order of A.D.M.S. (message 499 of date) 5 Sick admitted during the period up to time of present orders. | |
| " 30 " | Orders of note. Appointments for current period in their A. Section Major KELSALL {Subadar GAURI SHANKAR . W.O. Dewa Singh 57R (one S.A.S.S.B.M.) " Yusef Khan 17.1 P.S. Havildar Ahmed Khan 59 R. B. Section Major BROWSE {Jemadar NAMAK CHAND W.O. Nur Mohd 59R 3rd class SAS SURAS PAL " Mohkat Singh 16 R. P.S. Havildar Kishen Chand 22 P. C. Section Captain BOYD {1st class SAS. NARAIAN W.O. Sajawal Khan 62 P PARSHAD SOKOL 3rd class SAS. ALI JAN " Bhur Singh 3H P.S. Havildar Punjab Singh 59R. D. Section Captain KENNEDY {2nd class SAS ANANT W.O. Rattan Singh 8 R PARAB " Sadu Singh 431 3rd class SAS. GOKHAL SINGH P.S. Havildar Charman Singh 47 S. | |

Army Form C. 2118.

# WAR DIARY
## or
## INTELLIGENCE SUMMARY.
(Erase heading not required.)

Page 45.

| Hour, Date, Place | Summary of Events and Information | Remarks and references to Appendices |
|---|---|---|
| Sept 30. Croix Barbuse 1915 | Appointments notified (Continued)<br><br>Bearer Company. Captain BOYD<br>"  " Captain KENNEDY<br><br>Subedar GAURI SHANKAR – SAS. ALI JAN – GOKHAL SINGH – SURAJ PAL<br><br>W.Os RATTAN SINGH – BUR SINGH – YUSAF KHAN – MOHAT SINGH.<br>Bhistis. Nama – Bhagwan Din<br>Cooks. Man Din – Mehabir<br>Sweepers. Bhondu – Alla Ditta.<br><br>Weather. Up to 24th the weather was exceptionally bright & warm<br>from 24th inclusive it became wet and cold.<br><br>                                     [signature]<br>                                     O.C. III F.A. | |

Serial No. 154

F. Oct 1915

Confidential

121/7601

War Diary

of

No. 112 Indian Field Ambulance.

FROM 1st October 1915. TO 31st October 1915.

Army Form C. 2118.

# WAR DIARY
## or
## INTELLIGENCE SUMMARY.
*(Erase heading not required.)*

Pages 47 — 52

112 Indian Field Ambulance

LAHORE DIVISION

October 1915

| Hour, Date, Place | Summary of Events and Information | Remarks and references to Appendices |
|---|---|---|

# WAR DIARY or INTELLIGENCE SUMMARY

Army Form C. 2118. Page 47

| Hour, Date, Place | Summary of Events and Information | Remarks and references to Appendices |
|---|---|---|
| October 1, 1915. CROIX MARMUSE | Quiet day. No shells fired. | |
| " 2. " | Nitts 2.0 G.B.C. km & (Much Direct) 7a S. Voast to Nulu (about 8.30 pm) shells under bylm tenced & Lt. Withrove R.S.C. | |
| " 3. " | Nitts (messay 50 B. 2.10.15) the limit marched to LA GORGUE & took up billets in the school formerly occupied & opened for sick at World of the Division. (10.45am to noon). Capt. BOYD & S.A.S. Surg. Rev. wrote 24 tucher, equipment & heard established took over the actual & dressing section at S. Voast at 10.0 A.M. The cura guides more over an advanced dressing station at the "Open Barn" run by the B.F.A. open with their personnel at a similar station at S. Voast run by the 1st F.A. open with a S.A.S. out Sidney. - A.B.C. km & heard Establishment. the power along the ail posts E N S including the ESTAIRES LA-BASSEE road is the Quitter ain posts W of this road. One Officer from every the truth in turn takes a 24 hour tour of duty. Serving up on the front & — 10.0 AM to 10.0 A.M. Admitted 24 Sick 21 admitted up to 9.0 A.M. on 4. | Map France ("B" Series) 36 A. 1/40,000 |
| " 4 La Gorgue L 34 B. 10.3 | Major HELSALL prouced 7a S. Voast for tour of duty off P.J. de SOUZA M.S. officer to arrived for duty. Would 11 Sick 11 admitted during the 24 hours. | e.c.h. |

# WAR DIARY or INTELLIGENCE SUMMARY.

Army Form C. 2118.

Page 46.

(Erase heading not required.)

| Hour, Date, Place | Summary of Events and Information | Remarks and references to Appendices |
|---|---|---|
| October 5. La Gorgue 1915 | Quietly to rute. 65 wded S.Voast 3.0 PM & fit all runy. | |
| " 6 | Wounded 9 Sick 17 admitted during the 24 hrs. Captain Boyd & Lt de Sousa (latter for instruction) proceeded to S.Voast for 24 hrs. tour of duty at 9.30 AM. Sentence of C.S.G.Ch on No 473 Sepoy Shah hawaz (patient in the 129ᵗʰ B. Infidel) promulgated in presence of Ambulance Staff at 9.0 AM. Wounded 11 Sick 21 admitted during the 24 hours up to 9.0 AM 7ᵗʰ | |
| " 7 | Quietly to rute. Wounded 3 Sick 6 admitted during the 24 hrs, up to 9.0 am 8ᵗʰ | |
| " 8 | Captain Kennedy proceeded to S.Voast for 24 hrs tour of duty 9.30 AM Wounded 4 Sick 14 admitted up to 9.0 AM 9ᵗʰ Quietly to rute. | |
| " 9 | Wounded 10 Sick 7 admitted up to 9.0 AM 10ᵗʰ Lieut de Sousa proceeded to S.Voast for 24 hrs tour of duty at 9.30 AM Wounded 2 Sick 14 admitted during the 24 hours. | |
| " 10 | Quietly to rute. Wounded 17 hm. hm. 7 wnded 24 sick admitted during the 24 hrs. Part II orders. M1/07749 Pte B.E. HARDING to rest FAWO. | |
| " 11 | Major Kelsall proceeded to S.Voast for 24 hrs tour of duty at 9.30 AM Quietly to rute. 14 wounded 3 sick admitted during the 24 hrs. | |
| " 12 | | |

Army Form C. 2118.

Page 49

# WAR DIARY
## or
## INTELLIGENCE SUMMARY.
(Erase heading not required.)

| Hour, Date, Place | Summary of Events and Information | Remarks and references to Appendices |
|---|---|---|
| 1915<br>Jun 13. LA GORGUE | Nothing to note. | |
| " 14th | Part II orders. 2nd Class Senior SAS NANAK CHAND ANAND transferred sick yesterday.<br>No 2629 Sepy W.O. Phugga Singh reported arrived yesterday.<br>60 wounded 11 sick admitted during the 24 hours. | |
| " 15th | Captain BOYD proceeded to S.Voast at 9.30 AM for the 24 hours routine duty.<br>4 wounded 19 sick admitted<br>Nothing to note. | |
| " 16th | 6 wounded 12 sick admitted.<br>Captain Kennedy proceeded to S.Voast at 9.30 AM for the 24 hours routine duty. | |
| " 17th | 5 wounded 10 sick admitted<br>Nothing to note.<br>2 wounded 9 sick admitted | |
| " 18th | L/Cpl de SOUSA proceeded to S.Voast at 9.30 AM for the 24 hours routine duty.<br>8 wounded 18 sick admitted | |
| " 19th | Part II orders. Staff Sergt. Pvn. MUGFORD SGT reported his arrival as S/Sgt Sergt in place of S/Sgt WATKINS sick in England.<br>Nothing to note 2 wounded 7 sick admitted | |
| " 20 — | Major HELSALL proceeded to S.Voast at 9.30 AM for the 24 hr. routine duty.<br>4 wounded 6 sick admitted. | AS |

# WAR DIARY or INTELLIGENCE SUMMARY

Army Form C. 2118.

Page 50.

| Hour, Date, Place | Summary of Events and Information | Remarks and references to Appendices |
|---|---|---|

**October 21, LA GORGUE.** — Nothing of note. 5 wounded 4 Sick admitted during the 24 hours.

**22** — Under instructions from A.D.M.S. (message 546. 20.10.05) the O.C. handed over the S Veust post to the Inniskill Divn at 10.0 A.M. A conbined British & Indian advanced post formed into No7 B.F.A. at M 27 c 1.73 ("Green Barn") to clear the area Dimil from extending from Crescent farm to Sunken Rd. An Assist Surg with necessy equipment and personnel to British side & wanted at a Sub Assist Surg— with the Same In Indian. 4 lucrius left at each regimental aid post as began to help in armed to evacuate cases as they occur. A B.O. to be detailed on alternate days from the B & I F.As to visit the post or satisfy himself that all satisfacty. If the above arrangets working smoothly.

Captain Boyd visited the post and and parks during the afternoon to make in the position of the latter and want not where any changes would be made in the course of the changes during the night.

Part II orders. No 379 3rd class S.A.S. G.R. RANE of late his cenns from 111 I.F.A. for keeping duty if fit only. No 1046 1st class S.A.S. KARIM BAKHSH attd from— 113 I.F.A. in this stead. 3 hunded 5 Sick admitted

**23** — Reguard aid posts taken up during the night definitely presented by an Officer of No7 on a Spot map Sent to A.D.M.S. 3 wonded 9 Sick admitted SAS Nawab Chand Sick

Part II orders. S.A.S. Ali Jan Atached to B Section & to be under— of an Officer

Army Form C. 2118.

Page 51

# WAR DIARY
## or
## INTELLIGENCE SUMMARY.
*(Erase heading not required.)*

| Hour, Date, Place | | Summary of Events and Information | Remarks and references to Appendices |
|---|---|---|---|
| 1915 Oct 24. LA GORGUE. | | Captn Kennedy proceeded to the Green Barn at 9.30 AM All satisfactory. Regimental aid posts visited. 6 wounded 3 Sick admitted. | |
| " 25 " | | 6 wounded 12 Sick admitted. | |
| " 26 " | | Capt de SOUSA proceeded to the Green Barn at 9.30 AM all satisfactory 11 wounded 14 Sick admitted | |
| " 27 " | 9.30 PM | A high explosive shell burst between the two huts ambulance parked inside the Green Barn. Ambulance & Men went out a good deal of the bodywork smashed but came in under its own power. the No 7 R.F.A. Ambulance had some injuries to the engine & was stored in by the FA.W.W. Drivers Lindley was in the bivouac at the time. 7 wounded 24 Sick admitted. O.C. visited Green Barn. | |
| " 28 " | | Major KELSALL visited the Green Barn & Quinine injection aid posts as there was a change of Brigades. 2 wounded 10 Sick admitted Surg General W.G. MACPHERSON C.B. visited the Unit in the afternoon | |
| " 29 " | | Quiet day & night. 3 wounded 18 Sick admitted | |
| " 30 " | | Captain BOYD visited the Green Barn. All satisfactorily. 2 wounded 13 Sick admitted | |
| " 31 " | | Quiet day & night. 2 wounded 19 Sick admitted | |

Army Form C. 2118.

Page 52

# WAR DIARY
## or
## INTELLIGENCE SUMMARY.
*(Erase heading not required.)*

| Hour, Date, Place | Summary of Events and Information | Remarks and references to Appendices |
|---|---|---|
| LA GORGUE. Oct 31. | Weather during the month.<br>1st to 3rd fine<br>4 to 10th dull cold wet wet<br>11 to 13 fine & Sunny.<br>14 to 18 dull & cold some rain.<br>19-20 fine & Sunny<br>21. dull & very cold.<br>22.23 fine. 24 to 31. had cold & dull. | C J B[?]<br>O.C. 1R.F.A. |

Army Form C. 2118.

# WAR DIARY
## *or*
## INTELLIGENCE SUMMARY.
*(Erase heading not required.)*

Instructions regarding War Diaries and Intelligence Summaries are contained in F.S. Regs., Part II. and the Staff Manual respectively. Title pages will be prepared in manuscript.

Pages 53

112 Indian Field Ambulance

LAHORE DIVN

November 1915

COMMITTEE FOR THE
4 NOV 1919
MEDICAL HISTORY OF THE WAR

Army Form C. 2118.

# WAR DIARY
## or
## INTELLIGENCE SUMMARY.
(Erase heading not required.)

Page 53.

| Hour, Date, Place | Summary of Events and Information | Remarks and references to Appendices |
|---|---|---|
| November 1st LA GORGUE. | Captain Kennedy visited the Green Barn M 27 d at 9.30 AM. All cases on return parade held there. Admitted W.1. Sick 21 | Maps FRANCE (B Series) Bethune 1/40,000 |
| Nov 2 - do | Lt De Souza visited the Green Barn. Admitted W 3 Sick 18 | |
| Nov 3rd do LA GORGUE | Admissions W. 6 Sick 10. | |
| Nov 4 do — | CAPT A. Souza left this unit to join Working Battalion Major T L Kinham joined this unit from the Working Battalion. Admissions W 2. Sick 23 | |
| Nov 5 do — | Major Browne IMS left on Short Leave.(1week) Capt Coyd IMS. visited the Green Barn. Major Kelsall IMS took over the duties of Maj Browne IMS during his absence Admissions W 1. S.5 | |
| Nov 6 do | Admissions W 0. Sick 19 & | |
| Nov 7 do | Major Kinham visited the Green Barn. Admissions W 2 S 36 | |

# WAR DIARY
## or
## INTELLIGENCE SUMMARY.
*(Erase heading not required.)*

Army Form C. 2118.

Instructions regarding War Diaries and Intelligence Summaries are contained in F.S. Regs., Part II and the Staff Manual respectively. Title pages will be prepared in manuscript.

| Hour, Date, Place | Summary of Events and Information | Remarks and references to Appendices |
|---|---|---|
| Nov 8. La Gorgue | Under orders from A.D.M.S. one British Officer (Capt Bird) with the following personnel took over charge of the Green Barn with the addition of personnel personnel from No 7 B7a to form a detached unit for the regiments of Lahore Div. which were left in the trenches to wit of the rest of the Division was on the move. <br><br> Personnel <br> 2 Sub asst Surgeons. <br> one P.S. Havildar <br> 2 W. orderlies. <br> 1 Cook <br> 2 Sweepers <br> 1 bearer <br><br> There were two Mo Tor Ambulances & one kit to relief detached from this unit to remain with the detached unit. The rest were evacuated direct to C.C.S. <br> The unit marched at 11 a.m. from La Gorgue to Jean En Artois via Merville, St Venant to Gonbecq marching in rear of the Ferozepore Brigade. Billets not at La |  |

Army Form C. 2118.

# WAR DIARY
## or
## INTELLIGENCE SUMMARY.
*(Erase heading not required.)*

Instructions regarding War Diaries and Intelligence Summaries are contained in F. S. Regs., Part II. and the Staff Manual respectively. Title pages will be prepared in manuscript.

| Hour, Date, Place | Summary of Events and Information | Remarks and references to Appendices |
|---|---|---|
| Nov 8. Could | 027a to 027c 3.6. The unit arrived at the new area about 5 p.m. — No admissions. The unit is now closed. | |
| Nov 9. Hamsin Outhu | Capt A Kennedy IMS left for temporary duty with 89th Punjabis. 4 ambulances with 16 mules, & 6 European drivers joined this unit | |
| Nov 10 — do — | Returned 26 heavy draught horses & got in exchange 30 mules. | |
| Nov 11 — do — | Capt Bora & two detached section reported this unit. All mules & officers chargers booked for Flanders. | |

(73989) W4141—463. 400,000. 9/14. H.&J.Ltd. Forms/C. 2118/10.

Army Form C. 2118.

# WAR DIARY
## or
## INTELLIGENCE SUMMARY.
(Erase heading not required.)

O 56

Instructions regarding War Diaries and Intelligence Summaries are contained in F.S. Regs., Part II and the Staff Manual respectively. Title pages will be prepared in manuscript.

| Hour, Date, Place | Summary of Events and Information | Remarks and references to Appendices |
|---|---|---|
| Ham en Artois, Nov 12. 1915 | Cables closed. Maj- G. (BROWSE) reported arrival fr Short Leave R KEESALL " departure date | Maps FRANCE (B series) Sheet 36 A 1/40,000 |
| " 13 | Nothing of note. | |
| " 14 | SAS. Karim Bakhsh reported his departure to Lucc 113 IEA | |
| " 15 | Nothing of note. | |
| " 16 | SAS. G.H.R RANE taken in strength of Unit permanently. Nothing of note. | |
| " 17 | Nothing of note. | |
| ENGUINEGATTE 18 | The Unit marched to ENGUINEGATTE via Maringhem (Blossy) from the Terrosebere Rd, from local information at the last place I was told the direct good through M 10 to 13 C was impossible for transport so made a detour via Heuches. Time 10.30 AM to 4.0 PM. Transport much satisfactory considering muddy and driverless stage to one another at times the first move of the unit under the new conditions. Billets in various parts of village widely separated otherwise satisfactory. Unit closed. Captain Boyd reported departure on Short Leave. Nothing of note. | |
| " 19 | Maj- J.L. Lonham reported departure on Short Leave. Nothing of note. | |
| " 20 | Captain A Kennedy reported arrival fr-69 Punjabis for duty. Major Riversdale reported arrival from Short Leave. Nothing of note. | |
| " 21 | Nothing of note. | |
| " 22 | | |
| " 23-24 | Nothing of note. Apr 24. Nov 12 b, 1 class SAS. Parmanand Sharma reported On arrival fr- III IIEA for permanent duty. | |
| " 25 | Captain A. Kennedy reported departure on Short Leave. | |

Army Form C. 2118.

P 57.

# WAR DIARY
## or
## INTELLIGENCE SUMMARY.
(Erase heading not required.)

Instructions regarding War Diaries and Intelligence Summaries are contained in F.S. Regs., Part II. and the Staff Manual respectively. Title pages will be prepared in manuscript.

| Hour, Date, Place | Summary of Events and Information | Remarks and references to Appendices |
|---|---|---|
| ENGUINEGATTE Nov 26. 1915 | Nothing of note. | |
| " 27 | ditto Captain Boyd separate Unit for short leave. | |
| " 28 | Major Browne proceeded on short leave. Lt. Bias IMS reported arrival from Lahore Indian Gen. Hosp. for duty. Major Dunlan reported from leave. | |
| Beaumetz-les-Aire Nov 29 | Marched from Enguinegatte via Petignay Mbanny to Beaumetz les Aire. On arrival, that night, installed & open for sick of Division. | |
| " Nov 30 | Capt Boyd IMS left the Unit for duty at Lahore Indian General Hospital. New Admissions / Sick 32 Admitted Transfers from No 113 TFA. II. | |
| | Weather during the month was wet 8 cold on 26-27/11/25 the was some frost. | |

O.S.Spew
O.C. 113 T.F.A.

112 3rd Field Ambulance.

John Dix

Dec. 1915.

Dec. 1915.

(6414) Wt. W3906/P1607 2,500,000 7/18 McA & W Ltd (E 3591) Forms W3091/4.     Army Form W.3091.

# Cover for Documents.

**Nature of Enclosures.**

Salonica    X-Ray

History 18th

---

**Notes, or Letters written.**

Army Form C. 2118.

# WAR DIARY
## or
## INTELLIGENCE SUMMARY.

*(Erase heading not required.)*

Pages 58—60

112 Indian Field Ambulance

Lahore Division

December 1915

COMMITTEE FOR THE
4 NOV 1949
MEDICAL HISTORY OF THE WAR

Army Form C. 2118.

P58.

# WAR DIARY
## or
## INTELLIGENCE SUMMARY.
*(Erase heading not required.)*

| Hour, Date, Place | Summary of Events and Information | Remarks and references to Appendices |
|---|---|---|
| Beauval, les Aires Dec 1st/15 | marched at 9-45 a.m. via Laires & Febvin Palfort to Auxettes — Admissions 2.3 Sick | gone to sick at Isles Trpts of Divn |
| Auxettes. Dec 2. | Admitted 13 Sick | |
| " Dec 3 | Lt. Dias IMS sent in to No 6 BFA Sick Admitted 11 Sick | |
| " 4 | Captn KENNEDY rejoined fr — last leave. Admitted 29 Sick | |
| " 5 | Admitted 1 mule " 11 Sick | |
| " 6 | Major BROWSE rejoined fr last leave Admitted 23 Sick | |
| " 7 | Admitted 1 mule. admitted 10 Sick | |
| " 8 | Admitted 1 mule " 6 Sick | |
| " 9 | Admitted 1 mule " 12 Sick | |
| " 10 | Major KELSALL reported attachment on special duty under orders Div fADMS admitted 26 Sick | |
| " 11 | Admitted 1 mule " 10 Sick cut. | |

**WAR DIARY** or **INTELLIGENCE SUMMARY.**
(Erase heading not required.)

Army Form C. 2118.
Page 59.

| Hour, Date, Place | Summary of Events and Information | Remarks and references to Appendices |
|---|---|---|
| Dec 12. 1915 AMETTES | Recd. orders to move to LILLERS on 13th in two parties to adv.... | |
| 13. " | Two sections under Major BROWSE left Cillers 3.15 AM arrival LILLERS 5.45 AM all vehicles & personnel on train by 7.30 AM. Two sections under Major LONHAM left Cillers at 5.0 AM arriving LILLERS at 6.0 AM. Vice ......... animals and other charges left behind to come on under Staff Sergt. ......... Train ......... Had first ordinary ... | |
| 14. " | Arriv. 1.30. S.S. transport to meet us all cooks & ambulance wagons Had to be dragged by hand from the siding to the ship and 1/4 mile all personnel & baggage embarked by 5.30 PM. Sect 1 (under Major Lonham and ... at 5.0 PM. Party also dragged their cart up from the station. All on board by 10.30 PM. All wagon park (still 112 (IFA at left with embarkation staff), only two water carts taken in their | |
| 15. MARSEILLES | Vessel S.S. NILE (Pacific Mail S.S. Co) Took on crew dock ... Ordnance (4 Maxims 36 ... ) & loaded ... old ones (4 operatic Maxims foreigns ... a ... the original ... battery was on the Cutter has in unserviceable been in use ... the Company | |
| 16. " | | |
| 17/18 " | Sailed 11.0 AM. Heavy swell. All personnel sea sick ... | |

Army Form C. 2118.

Page 60.

# WAR DIARY
## or
## INTELLIGENCE SUMMARY.
*(Erase heading not required.)*

Instructions regarding War Diaries and Intelligence Summaries are contained in F.S. Regs., Part II. and the Staff Manual respectively. Title pages will be prepared in manuscript.

| Hour, Date, Place | Summary of Events and Information | Remarks and references to Appendices |
|---|---|---|
| Dec 19, Voyage | Heavy swell, personnel still seasick | |
| 20, " | ditto | |
| 21, " | Calm | |
| 22, " | Reached Alexandria 5.0 pm | |
| 23, " | Alexandria 5.0 pm. Arrived Port Said 6.0 am 24th Dec | |
| 25, " | Left 10.0 am and Ismailia 7.0 pm. Anchored for the night. | |
| 26, " | And Suez. Sailed at dusk. | |
| 27, " | Red Sea. Cool. 26th – Following wind, lay lat 85° in shade. | |
| 29 | Hot Some breeze. 30 & 31st Cooler. | |

(73989) W4141—463. 400,000. 9/14. H.&J.Ltd. Forms/C. 2118/10.

www.ingramcontent.com/pod-product-compliance
Lightning Source LLC
Chambersburg PA
CBHW081427160426
43193CB00013B/2207